Pathfinders

Weather

WELDON OWEN
PUBLISHING

Contents

Weather Patterns 6

Wild Weather 28

Watching the Weather 46

Pathfinders

Weather

Conceived and produced by Weldon Owen Pty Limited
59 Victoria Street, McMahons Point, NSW, 2060, Australia
A member of the Weldon Owen Group of Companies
Sydney • San Francisco • Auckland • London

WELDON OWEN PUBLISHING
Chairman: John Owen
Publisher: Sheena Coupe
Art Director: Sue Burk
Consultant, Design Concept and Cover Design: John Bull
Design Concept: Clare Forte, Robyn Latimer
Editorial Assistants: Sarah Anderson, Kiren Thandi
Editorial Coordinator: Tracey Gibson
Production Manager: Caroline Webber
Vice President International Sales: Stuart Laurence
European Sales Director: Vanessa Mori

Author: Scott Forbes
Consultant: Richard Whitaker
Project Editor: Stephanie Goodwin
Designer: Lena Lowe
Picture Research: Joanna Collard

Illustrators: Richard Bonson/Wildlife Art Ltd, Robin Bouttell/Wildlife Art Ltd, Anne Bowman,
Chris Forsey, Richard McKenna, Nicola Oram, Oliver Rennert, Glen Vause

Maps: Laurie Whiddon

Color Reproduction by Colourscan Co Pte Ltd
Printed by Tien Wah Press Pte Ltd
Printed in Singapore

ISBN 978-1-74089-551-4

10 9 8 7 6 5 4 3

A WELDON OWEN PRODUCTION

Pick Your Path!

IMMERSE YOURSELF in the world around you—it's time to get weather-wise. Start at the beginning and learn about the ocean of air we live in and the sun that fuels our weather. Read through to the Little Ice Age and discover skaters on a frozen River Thames. Or, for the more adventurous, jump into "Thunderstorms," "Twisters" or "Floods," and move through the Wild Weather pages.

You'll find plenty of other discovery paths to choose from in the special features sections. Read about real-life storm chasers in "Inside Story," or get creative with "Hands On" activities. Delve into words with "Word Builders," or amaze your friends with fascinating facts from "That's Amazing!" You can choose a new path with every reading—PATHFINDERS will take you wherever *you* want to go.

INSIDE STORY
In the Extreme

Take a ride through the eye of a hurricane with the 53rd Weather Reconnaissance Squadron. Learn how Glaisher and Coxwell made their world-record ascent in a hot-air balloon. Read how Mario Molina and Sherwood Rowland predicted a hole in the ozone layer over ten years before its discovery. INSIDE STORY introduces you to the men and women who have shaped the past, present and future of meteorology.

HANDS ON
Create and Make

Create your very own indoor lightning display. Learn how to split and reflect light to create a rainbow. Construct your own kit of instruments to record air pressure, rainfall and wind speed, and create your own weather journal. Perfect for a rainy day, HANDS ON features experiments, projects and activities, each one related to that page's main subject.

Word Builders

What a strange word! What does it mean? Where did it come from? Find out by reading *Word Builders*.

That's Amazing!

Awesome facts, amazing records, fascinating figures— you'll find them all in *That's Amazing!*

Pathfinder

Use the *Pathfinder* section to find your way from one subject to another. It's all up to you.

Ready! Set! Start exploring!

Weather Patterns

WHEREVER YOU LIVE, it's likely that one of the first things you do each day is look outside to check the weather. The weather affects almost every aspect of our lives, from what we wear, to what we grow in our gardens. But what exactly is weather? Put simply, it's the movement of air over the surface of Earth. This brings cloud and wind, rain and snow. Although the weather may seem unpredictable, it is influenced by regular patterns, so that we experience much the same weather from year to year—a long-term weather pattern known as climate.

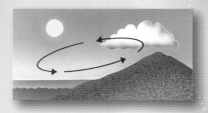

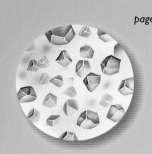

The Weather Zone

YOU MAY NOT REALIZE it, but you live in an ocean of air. We call this ocean the atmosphere, and without it we could not survive. The atmosphere provides us with the oxygen we need to breathe and the water we drink. It protects us from the Sun's harmful rays and from space debris such as asteroids, meteors and old satellites. And it keeps our planet at just the right temperature— neither too hot nor too cold—for life to exist.

Like creatures that live on the seafloor, we inhabit the bottom of this ocean. Above us, the air temperature varies with height, creating five distinct layers within the atmosphere. Humans discovered these layers in the late 19th century, when intrepid scientists began to climb thousands of feet into the sky in hot-air balloons. Several of these pioneers observed that the air temperature and the oxygen level fell as they rose. But it was French scientist Teisserenc de Bort who first noted that the temperature stopped falling above a height of about 6 miles (10 km). De Bort realized that this change marked the beginning of a new atmospheric layer, which we now call the stratosphere.

Just like an ocean, the atmosphere has tides, currents and waves. These circulations combine with water vapor in the air to create weather. Approximately 99 percent of our weather occurs in the lowest layer of the atmosphere, where we live. This layer is known as the troposphere. This is the weather zone.

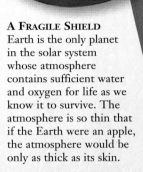

A FRAGILE SHIELD
Earth is the only planet in the solar system whose atmosphere contains sufficient water and oxygen for life as we know it to survive. The atmosphere is so thin that if the Earth were an apple, the atmosphere would be only as thick as its skin.

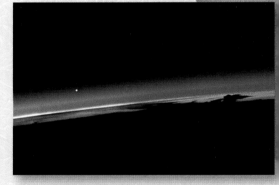

TOP OF THE TROPOSPHERE
The black shapes in this satellite picture of the atmosphere are thunderclouds. Usually, thunderclouds stop growing at the top of the troposphere, so their flat tops indicate the upper limit of the weather zone.

LAYER UPON LAYER
If you could soar slowly upward through the atmosphere clutching a thermometer, you would find that the temperature in the troposphere falls by about 4°F for every 1,000 feet (7°C for every 1,000 m). At the lower edge of the stratosphere, the air starts to warm up again, but in the next layer, the mesosphere, it cools once more. Things then heat up dramatically in the thermosphere and in the highest layer, the exosphere, where temperatures may top 3,000°F (1,650°C).

INSIDE STORY

By the Skin of Their Teeth

On September 5, 1862, five miles (8 km) above Wolverhampton, England, scientist James Glaisher calmly noted that his eyesight was failing. Glaisher was flying with his pilot Henry Coxwell. This was their second flight to study the upper atmosphere, and they had already passed the height reached on their first outing. But both men were now suffering from the extreme cold and the lack of oxygen. Glaisher asked Coxwell to help him read his instruments. But Coxwell had just noticed that the valve line, which had to be pulled to make the balloon descend, was tangled up above him in the rigging. When he climbed up to untangle it, he found that his hands were frozen and he could not lift them. In the meantime, Glaisher had passed out. If the balloon continued to climb, both men would die. With one last heroic effort, Coxwell managed to grasp the valve line with his teeth and pull it downward. As the balloon drifted to Earth, the two men recovered. They calculated that they had made a world-record ascent to more than 30,000 feet (9,150 m).

Word Builders

• **Atmosphere** comes from the Greek words *atmos*, meaning "vapor" or "gas," and *sphaera*, meaning "sphere."
• The top of the troposphere is the **tropopause**. Here the temperature is steady, or pauses, before rising.

That's Amazing!

• Without the effect of gravity, the gases that form the atmosphere would drift off into space.
• Opposing electrical charges in the thermosphere reflect radio waves. This allows us to bounce radio transmissions off the thermosphere to other parts of the globe.

Pathfinder

• Colorful displays of light known as auroras occur in the exosphere. Find out more on pages 26–27.
• Human activities may be damaging the ozone layer and overheating the atmosphere. See pages 60–61.

MAXIMUM PROTECTION

Certain gases in the atmosphere play a crucial role in making our planet habitable.

THE OZONE LAYER

Roughly 15 miles (24 km) above your head, there is a thin layer of a gas called ozone. Like a sunscreen, this layer shields us from harmful ultraviolet rays generated by the Sun.

THE GREENHOUSE EFFECT

The atmosphere lets light in and traps heat—just like a greenhouse. When sunlight enters the atmosphere, some is blocked by cloud. The rest is absorbed by Earth's surface or reradiated as heat. Gases called greenhouse gases prevent most of this heat escaping.

A BALANCING ACT

Different parts of Earth's surface reflect and absorb different amounts of sunlight. Oceans and tropical forests soak up large quantities, whereas icecaps reflect up to 90 percent of the sunlight that strikes them.

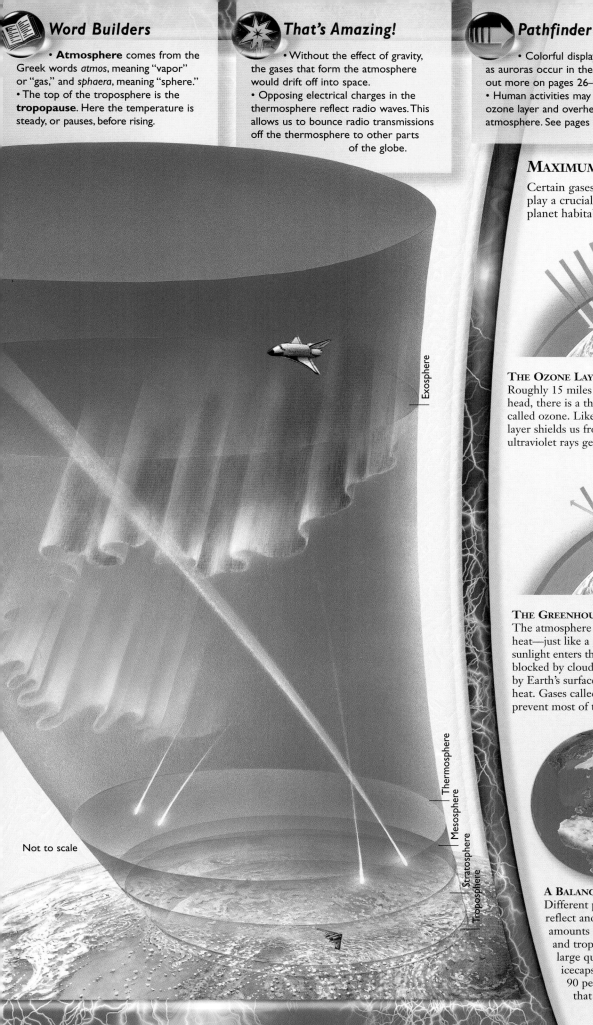

Exosphere

Thermosphere

Mesosphere

Stratosphere

Troposphere

Not to scale

Solar Powered

YOU PROBABLY KNOW that it gets hotter when the Sun comes out and cooler when it disappears. But did you know that the Sun causes winds to blow, clouds to form, and rain to fall? Did you realize that our weather is solar powered?

The atmosphere is made up of tiny, invisible air molecules. As a result of gravity, they press down on us continuously. They also buzz around constantly. Indeed, billions of them are bouncing off you right now as you read this. Together, these movements create what is known as air pressure, or atmospheric pressure.

When the Sun shines on Earth's surface, air molecules near the ground warm up and begin to rise. This process is called convection, and it forms an area of low pressure, or a low, on the ground. Eventually, the warm, rising air cools and spreads out. When it reaches a temperature cooler than its surrounds it begins to sink, forming an area of high pressure, or a high, some distance away from the low. Because the atmosphere tends to smooth out pressure differences, air then moves from the high to the low. We call this movement wind.

These processes occur all over the world, all the time. However, the Sun heats certain parts of our planet more than others and its strength varies from season to season. So the processes, and our weather, vary widely depending on the place and time of year.

INTO THIN AIR
Gravity pulls air molecules toward Earth's surface, so the higher you go the lower the air pressure and the amount of oxygen available. That's why climbers sometimes suffer from a shortage of oxygen.

Falling air prevents cloud formation

Sinking air creates high pressure

CAUGHT IN THE MIDDLE
The greater the pressure difference between two areas, the stronger the wind. So, if you feel a light breeze, you know you are somewhere between areas of moderately high and moderately low pressure. And if you are being blown off your feet, you know the pressure difference is very large indeed.

SEASONS CHANGE

Because Earth's axis is tilted at an angle of 23.5 degrees, the amount of solar energy reaching different parts of the globe varies as the planet orbits the Sun. These variations create our seasons. When a hemisphere is tilted toward the Sun, it is summer there and the days are at their longest. When it is tilted away from the Sun, it experiences winter and the days are at their shortest. In spring and fall, day and night are of a similar length and the weather is more temperate.

Northern spring, southern fall

Northern summer, southern winter

Northern fall, southern spring

Word Builders

• **Solar** means "of the Sun." The word comes from the Latin *solaris*, from the word for the Sun, *sol*.
• Air pressure is normally measured in **hectopascals**. This term combines the Greek word *hekaton*, meaning "100," and the surname of the French scientist and philosopher Blaise Pascal (1623–62). He was the first person to show that air pressure decreases with altitude. There are 100 pascals in a hectopascal.

That's Amazing!

• The air in an average-size room weighs about the same as a small child.
• The highest air pressure ever recorded at ground level measured 1083.8 hectopascals and occurred on December 31, 1968, in Siberia, Russia. The lowest ground-level pressure, of 877 hectopascals, was recorded at Guam in the Pacific Ocean in 1958.

Pathfinder

• The uneven heating of Earth by the Sun creates global patterns of air flow, which in turn give rise to major wind systems. See pages 12–13.
• Large weather systems that form around areas of low pressure can bring severe storms. See pages 16–17.
• Find out how rising air forms clouds on pages 22–23.
• See how weather maps show areas of high and low pressure on pages 56–57.

Air mass cools, spreads out, and sinks

Rising air encourages cloud formation

Wind blows from high to low pressure

Warm air rises, forming low pressure

L

HANDS ON

Under Pressure

❶ Blow up a balloon and hold the neck closed with your fingers. You have just created an area of high pressure inside the balloon. Now hold the neck of the balloon in front of your face and release your grip while still holding the balloon. The air rushes out of the balloon immediately, blowing air at your face. In the same way, air in the atmosphere moves from high pressure to low pressure, smoothing out the pressure difference and creating wind.

❷ Push a balloon into a wide bottle and stretch the neck around the top of the bottle. Ask a friend to blow up the balloon. No matter how hard they puff, they won't be able to blow it up. For a balloon to inflate, it must be able to expand and displace the air molecules around it. The air molecules inside the bottle cannot move, so the balloon cannot be inflated.

HIGHS AND LOWS

Warm air rises, reducing the number of air molecules at ground level and forming an area of low pressure. As it cools, it sinks, increasing the number of air molecules on the ground and forming high pressure. Air then moves from the high-pressure area toward the low-pressure area, creating wind. Rising air increases cloud formation, whereas sinking air prevents it. That's why low pressure normally brings cloudy, wet weather, and high pressure usually results in clear, sunny weather.

Northern winter, southern summer

HOT SPOT

Throughout the year, the Sun is strongest in the tropics. In June, it is directly above the Tropic of Cancer (left), and in December, it is over the Tropic of Capricorn (right).

Sailing ship

Weather vane

Global Air Flow

IF YOU CAN'T STAND THE HEAT, stay out of the tropics. All year long, the Sun beats down on this part of the globe. As a result, air rises steadily at the equator. It then spreads out, cools and sinks to the surface around 30 degrees north and south. From there, some air flows back toward the equator at ground level, completing a circular pattern of air flow called a cell. Similar cells exist between 30 and 60 degrees and between 60 degrees and the poles.

The movement of air at ground level within these cells creates Earth's major wind patterns. As the winds move north and south they are deflected by the planet's rotation: to the right in the northern hemisphere and to the left in the southern hemisphere. This effect was first explained in 1835 by a French scientist called Gustave-Gaspard de Coriolis, and it is known as the Coriolis Effect, in his honor.

The pattern of global air flow shapes our weather. For instance, the warm, moist air that rises at the equator results in humid conditions and regular heavy rainfall in the tropics. The sinking air at 30 degrees north and south of the equator creates a band of dry weather that has formed most of the world's deserts. And the westerly winds at around 40 to 60 degrees from the equator regularly carry wet and cloudy weather to North America and Western Europe.

Jet stream Strong, high-altitude, westerly winds

Hadley cell Warm air rises from the equator and spreads toward the poles before sinking at around 30 degrees north and south.

JET STREAMS
Powerful winds known as jet streams blow at high levels of the atmosphere between the major cells. If they carry moist air, they may form narrow bands of cloud, as seen in this satellite image of a jet stream over the Red Sea in North Africa.

WIND PATTERNS
Air circulations create three major types of cells. Those nearest the equator are called Hadley cells, for George Hadley, the English scientist who first described them in 1753. Ferrel cells, which circulate between 30 and 60 degrees and were first noted in 1856, are also named for their discoverer, American scientist William Ferrel. The cells at the poles are sometimes called polar Hadley cells.

Ferrel cell Some of the air from the Hadley cells continues toward the poles before rising at about 60 degrees north and south.

PARALLEL LINES
Take a close look at this satellite image and you'll see how rising air creates bands of cloudy, unsettled weather along the equator and above 40 degrees, while sinking air creates clearer skies near 30 degrees north and south.

Windmill

Word Builders

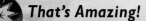

• The **trade winds** were named by early traders, whose sailing ships they pushed across the Atlantic Ocean.
• The **doldrums** were named by sailors who feared becoming stranded in this windless region. The name comes from an Old English word meaning "dull."

That's Amazing!

Jet streams can blow at up to 180 miles per hour (290 kph). When flying in the same direction, airline pilots sometimes hitch a ride on a jet stream. In North America, this can shorten a coast-to-coast flight by as much as an hour and a half. If a pilot flies against a jet stream, the speed of the plane may drop to that of a car on a freeway!

Pathfinder

• To find out why air flows from high to low pressure, go to pages 10–11.
• The Coriolis Effect causes winds to spiral around areas of low pressure. This can create large weather systems and even hurricanes. See pages 36–37.
• Learn about floods on pages 38–39.

TWISTING AND TURNING

As a result of the Earth's shape, the Coriolis Effect is strongest at the poles and nonexistent at the equator. In the northern hemisphere, it causes air to move clockwise and down around high pressure—like a screw going into wood—and anticlockwise and up around low pressure—like a screw being unscrewed. The movements are the opposite in the southern hemisphere.

Polar cell Cold air at the poles sinks and travels toward the equator before rising upon meeting the Ferrel cell.

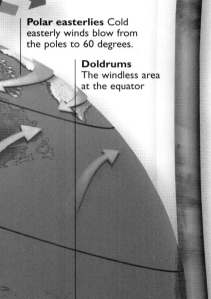

Polar easterlies Cold easterly winds blow from the poles to 60 degrees.

Doldrums The windless area at the equator

Trade winds Easterly winds blow toward the equator.

Westerlies Warm, moist winds blow from the west.

THE MONSOON

Patterns of global air flow influence local winds such as the monsoon. This seasonal wind brings heavy rain to many subtropical parts of the world, especially India and Bangladesh.

THE DRY SEASON

In winter, intense high pressure far inland creates northeasterly winds that push moist air away from India and Bangladesh, over the ocean.

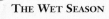

THE WET SEASON

Higher summer temperatures create low pressure in inland areas. This draws warm, moist air from over the ocean, resulting in torrential rain that often causes flooding.

Land and Sea

ON A HOT SUMMER'S day, why do so many people head for the coast? Partly, it's to enjoy a refreshing swim in the ocean. But it's also because coastal areas tend to be noticeably cooler when inland regions are sweltering. The explanation for this significant temperature difference lies in the contrasting heating and cooling properties of land and sea.

Landmasses warm up and cool down rapidly. So when the weather is hot, they get hot too, and when the weather turns cooler or night falls, they cool quickly. The sea, on the other hand, absorbs and releases heat slowly. And, unlike land, it's always on the move. This means that oceans can absorb heat in one place and release it in another, far away. So, where land and sea meet, a cold ocean current may cool the edge of a hot landmass or a warm current may heat a cold coastline.

The different properties of land and sea also give rise to coastal winds. On a warm day, for example, heating of the land causes air to rise rapidly, creating an area of low pressure. In turn, this draws air in from the sea, producing a steady, cool sea breeze—just what you need when the Sun is blazing!

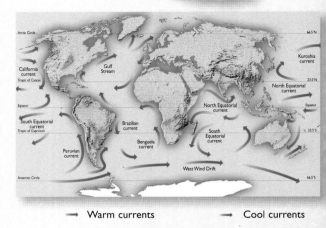

→ Warm currents   → Cool currents

HOT AND COLD RUNNING WATER

The major ocean currents are created by global wind patterns. They carry warm and cool water long distances around the globe and can strongly influence weather. A good example of this is the Gulf Stream, an ocean current that carries warm water from the Caribbean Sea to the North Atlantic Ocean. It makes the climate of northwestern Europe much milder than it would be otherwise.

 HANDS ON

The Water Cycle

1. Half-fill a wide, high-sided dish with a mixture of water and mud.

2. Place a glass at the center of the dish, with the open end up. The glass must be shorter than the sides of the dish.

3. Cover the dish with plastic wrap and place a pebble above the glass so the wrap dips at the center but does not touch the glass.

4. Leave the dish in a sunny place for several hours, then look in the glass. It should contain clean water. Heat from the Sun caused the water in the dish to evaporate, leaving the mud behind. The water vapor turned back into liquid on the underside of the plastic, just as water vapor turns into rain, then dripped from the center of the plastic into the glass, just as clean rain falls from the sky.

Water evaporates and forms clouds

COASTAL WEATHER PATTERNS

During the day, the boundary between land and sea is often marked by a long line of clouds. That's because the land releases more heat than the sea, causing more air to rise. When sufficient moisture is present, clouds form readily. This rising air also produces local winds called land and sea breezes.

Word Builders

Mountain ranges receive more rain than other land areas because they force moist air upward, increasing cloud formation. Once an air mass has crossed a mountain range, it sinks and dries out. This creates an arid region behind the range called a **rain shadow**.

That's Amazing!

The most powerful land breezes on Earth occur in the Antarctic, where night-time low pressure draws ice-cold air down from the high plateau and out to sea. Winds in excess of 100 miles per hour (160 kph) can result.

Pathfinder

• Pressure differences between land and sea contribute to the formation of winds called monsoons. See page 13.
• Hurricanes are fueled by the sea but weaken as they strike land. See page 36.
• Find out how changes in ocean currents may cause drought on page 41.

THE WATER CYCLE

The interaction of the atmosphere, land and sea creates a cycle of moisture that shapes our weather and provides us with a continuous supply of fresh water. When the Sun heats the ocean, lakes and rivers, some of the water turns into a gas called water vapor. This process is known as evaporation. The water vapor forms clouds, which in turn produce rain. Some rain is absorbed by soil and plants, and the rest flows back to the sea via rivers and underground channels.

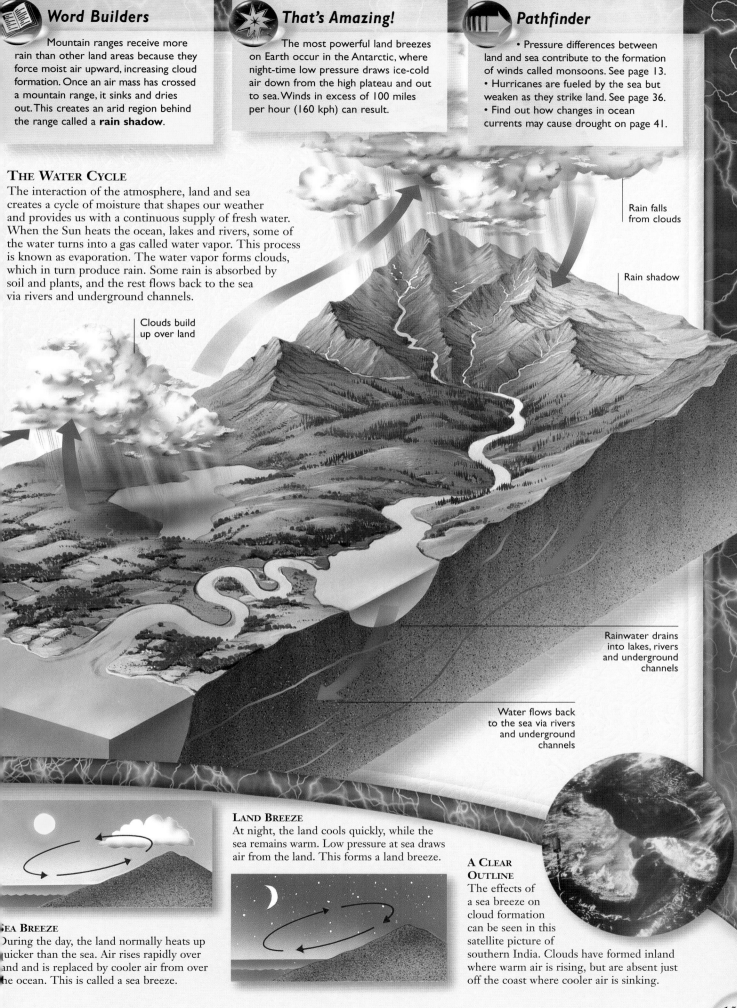

Clouds build up over land

Rain falls from clouds

Rain shadow

Rainwater drains into lakes, rivers and underground channels

Water flows back to the sea via rivers and underground channels

LAND BREEZE
At night, the land cools quickly, while the sea remains warm. Low pressure at sea draws air from the land. This forms a land breeze.

A CLEAR OUTLINE
The effects of a sea breeze on cloud formation can be seen in this satellite picture of southern India. Clouds have formed inland where warm air is rising, but are absent just off the coast where cooler air is sinking.

SEA BREEZE
During the day, the land normally heats up quicker than the sea. Air rises rapidly over land and is replaced by cooler air from over the ocean. This is called a sea breeze.

Cold front symbol　　　*Warm front symbol*

Frontal Systems

WHEN TWO AIR MASSES of different temperatures meet, they jostle for position along a boundary known as a front. These contests produce some of our wildest weather, especially in midlatitude zones.

The outcome of such a meeting depends on which way and how fast the air masses are traveling. When a moving cold air mass collides with a stationary warm air mass, the cold air drives under the warm air like a wedge, forcing the warm air upward. This creates a cold front. Because the warm air rises rapidly and steeply along the cold front, the temperature may change suddenly and large clouds and rain may form, resulting in wet, windy weather.

In contrast, when a moving warm air mass runs into a stationary cold air mass, the warm air rises gradually over the top of the cold air, forming a warm front. As the rising air moves at a shallower angle, temperature changes are slower and clouds and rain tend to spread over a wider area.

Sometimes, warm and cold air begin to spin around each other, forming a huge, spiraling air mass called a low-pressure system, or storm system. The rotation creates an area of low pressure at the center and two fronts, one warm and one cold. As the fronts rotate around the low-pressure area, they bring changeable and often stormy weather to a wide area. Low-pressure systems are most common in midlatitudes, where warm and cold air masses meet most frequently, and usually move eastward with prevailing winds.

HIGH ROTATION
In this satellite image of a low-pressure system, the cold front is a band of cloud extending from the center to the foreground. The warm front is within the cloud at the center.

WINDOW ONTO A STORM
The cross-section below shows a low-pressure system over Northern Europe. Its precise position is shown in the map above. The cold front is creating stormy conditions over western Europe. Farther east, a warm front is bringing light rain to a wide area of Poland. As the fronts move eastward, they can either strengthen or weaken depending on the nature of the low-pressure system.

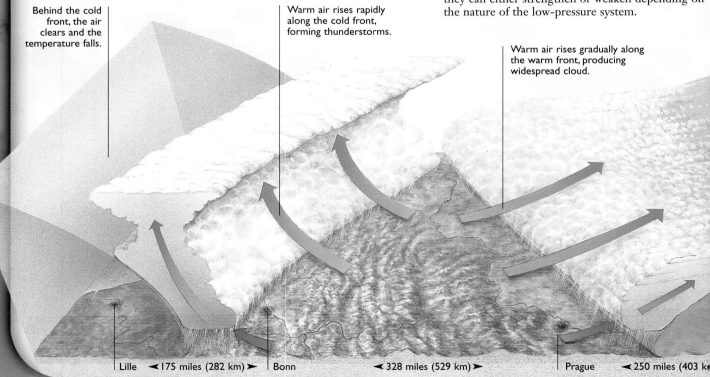

Behind the cold front, the air clears and the temperature falls.

Warm air rises rapidly along the cold front, forming thunderstorms.

Warm air rises gradually along the warm front, producing widespread cloud.

Lille ◄ 175 miles (282 km) ► Bonn ◄ 328 miles (529 km) ► Prague ◄ 250 miles (403 k

Word Builders

In the United States, a low-pressure system is also referred to as a **storm system**. In the United Kingdom and some other countries, it is sometimes called a **depression**.

That's Amazing!

A cold front brought the largest temperature change ever recorded in one day to Browning, Montana, in the United States, on January 23–24, 1916—a fall of 100 Fahrenheit degrees (56 Celsius degrees), from 44°F (7°C) to –56°F (–49°C).

Pathfinder

• In midlatitudes, low-pressure systems are carried eastward by prevailing winds. Find out more about major wind systems on pages 12–13.
• Fronts are marked on weather maps using the symbols shown opposite. Learn more on pages 56–57.

THE LEADING EDGE

The approach of a warm front is often signaled by the arrival of a broad band of high cirrus cloud. It is usually followed by altocumulus or altostratus, then thick, low-level stratus clouds. These frequently bring rain or, if the air temperature is low enough, snow.

INSIDE STORY

Breakthrough on the Polar Front

In 1917, a fierce war raged across Europe, cutting communications and weather networks. Without international cooperation, it seemed that little valuable research could be done. But in the Norwegian town of Bergen, a group of scientists, led by Vilhelm Bjerknes, used local data to examine what happened when cold air from the North Pole met warm air from the south. They soon realized that such encounters created much of the unstable weather found in northern Europe and that most of the activity occurred along the boundaries between the air masses. Bjerknes likened these to the battle zones of Europe and so called them "fronts." The Bergen School's research was a big breakthrough in the study of weather systems and helped improve the accuracy of forecasting in midlatitudes.

THE SPIN CYCLE

This series of diagrams shows how interaction between warm and cold air masses gives rise to a low-pressure or storm system.

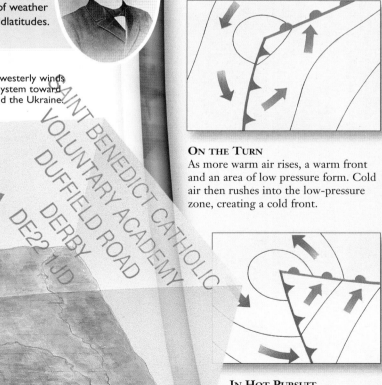

SIDE BY SIDE

Warm and cold air masses meet. A stationary front begins to form between them. At a certain point, some warm air starts to rise over the cold air.

ON THE TURN

As more warm air rises, a warm front and an area of low pressure form. Cold air then rushes into the low-pressure zone, creating a cold front.

IN HOT PURSUIT

The faster-moving cold front swings around toward the warm front. Eventually, it catches up with the warm front and cuts off the supply of rising air. The system then weakens.

reading cloud oduces light in and snow er Poland.

The leading edge of the warm front creates a band of high cloud.

Prevailing westerly winds push the system toward Belarus and the Ukraine.

Kraków ◄ 478 miles (771 km) ► Kiev

Climate

WEATHERWISE, NO TWO DAYS are ever exactly the same. But we generally experience similar weather from year to year. The pattern of weather that occurs in a region over an extended period of time is known as its climate.

Climate is influenced by a number of factors, including a region's latitude and altitude, prevailing winds and ocean currents. Landmasses near the poles have a cold climate, whereas those close to the equator are hot. Regions in-between are temperate, which means they are normally neither very hot nor very cold. Coastal areas usually have a less severe climate than continental, or inland, areas. Mountains tend to be cooler than nearby lowlands.

Climate has a direct effect on the kinds of vegetation that grow in different parts of the world. Warm, well-watered tropical regions have tall, dense forests, whereas hot, dry regions may have short, scrubby vegetation or even no plants at all. Climate also has a bearing on where humans live. The largest concentrations of people are found where the weather is neither too hot nor too cold, and where water, timber and fertile land are plentiful.

Northern Temperate

This zone forms a wi band below the Arcti Circle. Winters are long, cold and snowy. Summers are mild an wet. Anchorage, in Alaska (left), lies in this zone.

HANDS ON
Determining a Region's Climate

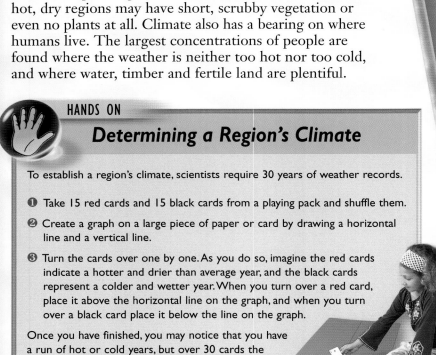

To establish a region's climate, scientists require 30 years of weather records.

❶ Take 15 red cards and 15 black cards from a playing pack and shuffle them.

❷ Create a graph on a large piece of paper or card by drawing a horizontal line and a vertical line.

❸ Turn the cards over one by one. As you do so, imagine the red cards indicate a hotter and drier than average year, and the black cards represent a colder and wetter year. When you turn over a red card, place it above the horizontal line on the graph, and when you turn over a black card place it below the line on the graph.

Once you have finished, you may notice that you have a run of hot or cold years, but over 30 cards the conditions average out. Similarly, 30 years is usually long enough to determine the average weather, or climate, of a region.

Rain forest

Desert

VEGETATION ZONES

Earth's climates form four broad bands of contrasting vegetation between the equator and the poles. High rainfall in tropical regions creates lush rain forests. Arid areas have little or no vegetation. Temperate climates give rise to deciduous forests or, in northern temperate areas, conifer forests. The polar regions are mostly covered by ice, but some areas have short trees and low-growing plants.

📖 Word Builders

• **Tropic** comes from the Latin *tropicus*, meaning "of the solstice." The solstice is when the Sun is at its highest or lowest point. In summer, the Sun is at its highest over the Tropic of Cancer (northern hemisphere) or the Tropic of Capricorn (southern hemisphere).
• The conifer forests of the northern temperate region are known as boreal forests. The word **boreal** comes from the Latin *boreas*, meaning "north wind."

✴ That's Amazing!

• The hottest place in the world is Dallol in Ethiopia, where the average temperature, over six years, was measured at 94°F (34°C).
• The coldest place is Oymyakon in Siberia, Russia, where the temperature recently fell to −98°F (−72°C).
• The temperature in the town of Verkhoyansk in Siberia, Russia, can range from as low as −90°F (−68°C) to a sweltering 98°F (37°C).

🏛 Pathfinder

• Climates are influenced by global air flow. See pages 12–13.
• Over millions of years, plants and animals have adapted to particular climates. Learn more on pages 44–45.
• The overall climate on Earth has changed many times over the past millions of years. Read about how scientists study long-term climate change on pages 58–59.

CLIMATE ZONES

Scientists divide the world's landmasses into climate zones—regions that experience similar kinds of weather. There are many different ways of classifying climates, but this map shows one of the most common systems. Note that the same type of climate can exist in widely separated parts of the world. For example, western California in the United States, southwestern Australia and southern Europe all have a Mediterranean climate.

Polar Regions around the North and South Poles have long, extremely cold winters and only slightly warmer summers. It snows often and can be very windy.

Temperate Temperate areas have four very distinct seasons and are neither very hot nor very cold. Winter is mild and wet and summer is warmer and drier.

Mountain Mountains are usually colder, wetter and windier than nearby lowland areas. They often receive heavy snowfalls in winter.

Mediterranean These zones, which include the lands that border the Mediterranean Sea, have hot, dry summers and cool, wet winters.

Arid These areas receive very little rain. Days are usually hot, but nights can be very cold. Winter may be bitterly cold.

Semiarid Temperatures are less extreme than in arid regions and slightly more rain falls. Conditions are generally warm and dry.

Tropical The weather in the tropics is hot and wet. It rains for most of the year, but there is usually a short dry season.

Subtropical Summers here are hot and almost as wet as in tropical areas. Winters tend to be drier and cooler.

:iduous
:st

Boreal forest

Tundra

Icecap

FOG CITY

The residents of San Francisco in the United States regularly wake to scenes like this. These fogs begin over the Pacific Ocean at night when warm air drifts over cold water and condenses. The following morning, as the land heats up, low pressure draws the fog into the bay and over the surrounding land.

Water in Many Guises

WATER IS A MASTER of disguise. As a gas, called water vapor, it is ever-present in the air around us, yet remains invisible. As a liquid, it forms rivers, lakes and oceans, and tumbles out of the sky as rain. As tiny droplets, it drifts in clusters as clouds. It can become solid overnight, turning puddles into sheets of ice. And it can materialize out of nowhere, appearing on the outside of a cold glass on a hot day, or on the bathroom mirror as you run a hot shower.

These transformations are the result of changes in the air's temperature and its humidity—the amount of water vapor it contains. Warm air can hold more water vapor than cold air. So, when moist air cools, it may no longer be able to hold all its water vapor. When this happens, the excess vapor turns to liquid. This is called condensation.

When water condenses on the ground, or another solid surface, at a temperature above freezing, it forms drops called dew. If the temperature is below freezing, the water turns into ice crystals, or frost.

In the air, water condenses onto microscopic particles of dust or salt. In freezing air, this produces tiny ice crystals. In warmer air, it creates tiny droplets. Large numbers of droplets or ice crystals make up cloud. When cloud forms near the ground it is called fog.

STEAMED UP

In a steamy bathroom, the air is very humid. When it makes contact with a cold surface, like a mirror, it condenses and forms drops of water.

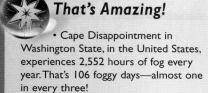 Word Builders

- **Hygrometer** comes from the Greek *hygros* meaning "wet."
- **Radiation** comes from *radius*, the Latin word for "ray."
- **Advection** is horizontal movement. The word comes from the Latin *advehere*, meaning "to carry to."

✴ That's Amazing!

- Cape Disappointment in Washington State, in the United States, experiences 2,552 hours of fog every year. That's 106 foggy days—almost one in every three!
- The particles on which water droplets condense in the air are less than a tenth of the width of a human hair.

Pathfinder

- Water turns into water vapor as a result of evaporation. See pages 14–15.
- Fog is just another name for cloud that forms on the ground. Learn more about clouds on pages 22–23.
- High humidity may be a sign of rain. Find out how forecasters measure humidity on pages 52–53.

THE FOG FAMILY

All kinds of fogs are the result of condensation, but we give them different names depending on how they happen.

ADVECTION FOG
If a fog forms as a result of warm, humid air moving over a cold surface, we call it advection fog. This type often occurs at the coast when sea air crosses cold land.

RADIATION FOG
When land cools rapidly, air immediately above it is chilled. If this air contains sufficient moisture, a radiation fog will form. Such fogs usually begin overnight.

FOG STRATUS
Fog clears when the Sun warms the air, causing the droplets to turn into vapor. If the ground warms quickly, the fog may clear from the bottom up, creating a band of fog just above the ground. This is called fog stratus.

✋ HANDS ON

Hair-Raising

Scientists measure humidity with a device called a hygrometer. You can make a simple hygrometer using human hair.

❶ Cut a wide triangular pointer out of a sheet of plastic or card. Attach a weight such as a small coin near the pointed end. Push a thumbtack through the wide end of the pointer.

❷ Stick the thumbtack and pointer onto thick cardboard or styrofoam, as shown below. Make sure the pointer moves freely.

❸ Attach the ends of three long strands of human hair to the center of the pointer. Then pin the other ends of the hairs to the top of the styrofoam or board, making sure that they are straight and that the pointer is perpendicular to the hairs.

When the air is humid, the hair will expand and the pointer will drop. When it is dry, the hair will shrink, causing the pointer to rise. You can test this by taking the hygrometer into a steamy bathroom. Mark the maximum humidity with an H for high. Then dry out the hair using a hair drier and mark the minimum with an L for low.

CRYSTAL CLEAR
On a freezing night, frost can form in one of two ways. Water vapor in the air may turn directly into ice crystals or surface water may freeze solid.

21

Cirrostratus

Clouds

BREATHE OUT SLOWLY on a cold day, and a cloud will form before your eyes. That's because the warm, moist air from inside your body cools rapidly in the cold air, and the moisture condenses to form a cluster of water droplets—a tiny cloud.

In the atmosphere, clouds form as the result of air rising and cooling, which in turn causes water vapor to change its state. If this happens in temperatures above freezing, the water vapor turns into liquid, or condenses. If it occurs below freezing, tiny ice crystals form. Some clouds are a mixture of water droplets and ice crystals.

Clouds come in a wide array of shapes, from puffy cotton-wool balls to great white streaks that stretch across the sky. In the early 19th century, an English amateur weather-watcher called Luke Howard devised a method of naming clouds. It defined three kinds: cumulus (puffy clouds), stratus (flat clouds) and cirrus (wispy clouds). To distinguish clouds at different heights, scientists use the prefixes alto- for middle-level clouds above 6,500 feet (2,000 m) and cirro- for high-level clouds above 16,500 feet (5,000 m). They also add other Latin terms to create more descriptive labels.

Human activities can create other types of clouds. For example, when aircraft fly through very cold air, the moisture from the engines' exhausts can freeze into tiny ice crystals, producing long clouds called contrails.

WHAT'S IN A NAME?

Clouds can form at any height, from just above ground level to the top of the troposphere. We name them according to their height and shape by combining the prefixes alto- and cirro- with the Latin names stratus (flat) and cumulus (puffy). (Low level clouds have no prefix.) Other Latin names are used to describe clouds in more detail. They include humilis (small or humble), undulatus (undulating or wavy) and fibratus (strand-like). So, high-level, flat clouds made up of thin strands can be called cirrostratus fibratus and middle-level, puffy, wavy clouds take the name altocumulus undulatus.

CIRRUS ABOVE
In this satellite image, cirrus clouds float high above a thick layer of stratus. Because the upper troposphere is freezing cold, cirrus clouds normally consist of ice crystals.

FLYING SAUCER
Strange disk-shaped clouds called lenticular clouds (altocumulus lenticularis) may form when air is pushed over mountains. Sometimes people mistake these clouds for UFOs!

INSIDE STORY

Hooked on Clouds

In the summer of 1783, volcanic eruptions in Japan and Iceland filled the atmosphere with ash, creating dramatic displays of color that highlighted the beauty of the clouds, and a fiery meteor streaked across the sky. From then on, eleven-year-old Luke Howard was hooked on weather. He studied, sketched and painted the skies over London and took regular scientific measurements of atmospheric conditions.

Late in 1802, Howard used his knowledge to create his own cloud classification scheme. A French scientist called Jean Baptiste Lamarck had already introduced a similar system, but Howard's had the advantage of being based on Latin, a language familiar to most scholars of the day. As a result, his system was soon adopted around the world.

Stratocumulus

Stratus

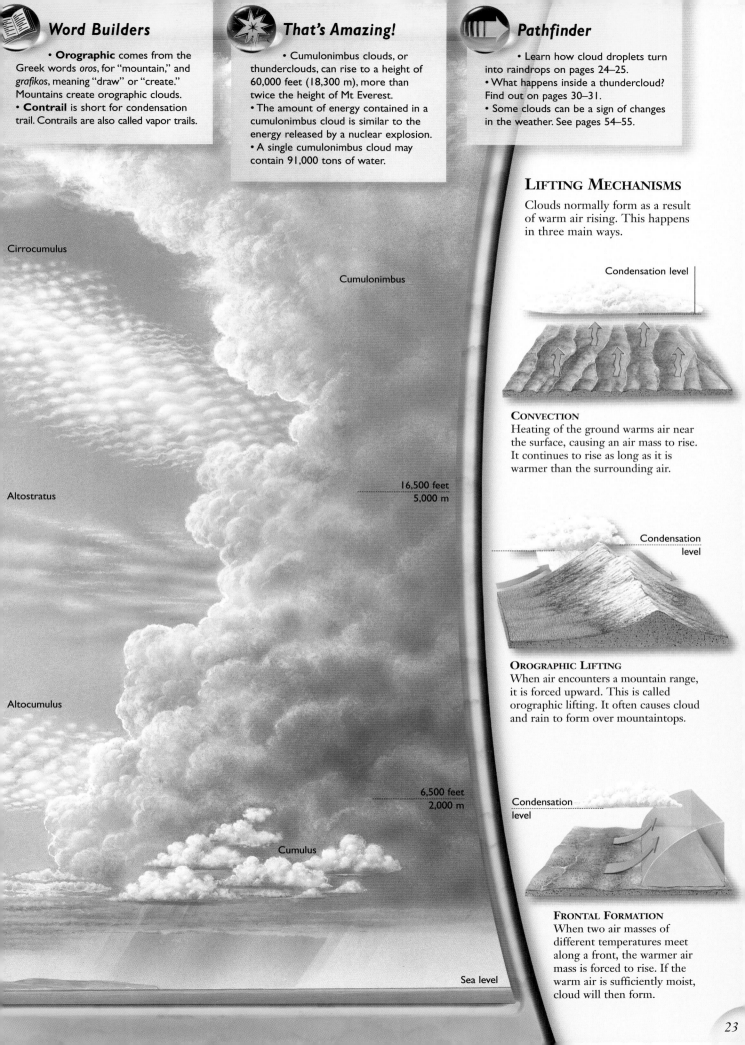

Word Builders

• **Orographic** comes from the Greek words *oros*, for "mountain," and *grafikos*, meaning "draw" or "create." Mountains create orographic clouds.
• **Contrail** is short for condensation trail. Contrails are also called vapor trails.

That's Amazing!

• Cumulonimbus clouds, or thunderclouds, can rise to a height of 60,000 feet (18,300 m), more than twice the height of Mt Everest.
• The amount of energy contained in a cumulonimbus cloud is similar to the energy released by a nuclear explosion.
• A single cumulonimbus cloud may contain 91,000 tons of water.

Pathfinder

• Learn how cloud droplets turn into raindrops on pages 24–25.
• What happens inside a thundercloud? Find out on pages 30–31.
• Some clouds can be a sign of changes in the weather. See pages 54–55.

Cirrocumulus

Cumulonimbus

Altostratus

16,500 feet
5,000 m

Altocumulus

6,500 feet
2,000 m

Cumulus

Sea level

LIFTING MECHANISMS

Clouds normally form as a result of warm air rising. This happens in three main ways.

Condensation level

CONVECTION
Heating of the ground warms air near the surface, causing an air mass to rise. It continues to rise as long as it is warmer than the surrounding air.

Condensation level

OROGRAPHIC LIFTING
When air encounters a mountain range, it is forced upward. This is called orographic lifting. It often causes cloud and rain to form over mountaintops.

Condensation level

FRONTAL FORMATION
When two air masses of different temperatures meet along a front, the warmer air mass is forced to rise. If the warm air is sufficiently moist, cloud will then form.

23

Precipitation

IF WATER DROPLETS and ice crystals in clouds grow large enough, they fall to Earth. Scientists refer to this falling water or ice as precipitation. We usually call it rain, snow or hail, depending on its form when it reaches the ground.

To turn into precipitation, water droplets and ice crystals have a good deal of growing to do. The average raindrop, for instance, is 100 times the diameter of a cloud droplet. Scientists think there are two main ways in which rain and snow form. The first, which is known as coalescence, occurs when water droplets are tossed around by wind within a cloud. As they bump into each other, they merge, or coalesce. Once they reach a certain size, they start to fall, and as they fall they strike other droplets and grow even larger. The second process occurs at temperatures near freezing, when water droplets stick to ice crystals, causing the crystals to grow until they are large enough to fall.

Hail is a little different. It occurs only within large cumulonimbus clouds fueled by powerful air currents. The currents carry ice crystals up and down within the cloud, causing layers of ice to build up around the original crystals. Eventually, when the hailstones become too heavy for the air currents to carry, they plummet to Earth.

In freezing cold air, water droplets stick to ice crystals. The crystals grow until they are large enough to fall.

In warmer air, water droplets collide and merge, or coalesce. Once the raindrops are large enough, they fall.

TYPES OF PRECIPITATION

A large cumulonimbus cloud can produce precipitation of all kinds. The type that lands on the ground depends on how it formed and how cold the air is between the cloud and the ground.

Rain

If the air below the cloud is above freezing, water droplets and ice crystals reach the ground as rain. If it is below freezing, ice crystals remain frozen and fall to the ground as snow or freezing rain.

INSIDE STORY

The Rainmaker

He referred to himself as the Moisture Accelerator, but most people called him the Rainmaker. Charles Hatfield of Oceanside, California, U.S.A., claimed to have discovered a method of increasing rainfall in 1902. In 1915, he offered to break a drought in San Diego for US$10,000. Days after he started work, rain began to fall. It poured for weeks. Dams overflowed, homes were flooded and bridges were washed away.

There was no real evidence that Hatfield had brought the rain. But that didn't prevent the city authorities blaming him, or Hatfield demanding his fee. Not surprisingly, he was never paid.

NAMES FOR THE RAINS

Rain can be described as heavy or light. The lightest form is called drizzle. Rain that evaporates before it lands on the ground is known as virga. Freezing rain is rain that turns to ice before it reaches the ground. Large cumulus clouds (left) tend to produce localized showers.

Thick stratiform clouds usually generate steady rain.

RAIN AND SNOW

Falls of rain and snow can be classified in different ways, depending on how long they last, how strong they are and in what form the precipitation is when it reaches the ground.

Word Builders

• In the United States, freezing rain is known as **sleet**. In the United Kingdom and Australia, this word refers to partially melted snow.

• **Virga** is a Latin word meaning "rod" or "streak." Virga forms streaks in the sky that stop short of the ground.

That's Amazing!

• The rainiest place in the world is Mount Waialeale in Kauai, Hawaii, which averages 350 wet days each year.

• The heaviest recorded hailstones fell on Bangladesh in 1986 and weighed 2 pounds (1 kg). They killed 92 people.

Pathfinder

• Thunderstorms are the source of hail. Find out more on page 30.

• Heavy rain can result in catastrophic floods. Turn to pages 38–39.

• Find out more about the shapes of snowflakes on pages 42–43.

Hail forms when ice pellets are swirled around within a cloud by air currents (shown as arrows). As the ice circulates, it collects moisture, which freezes to form layers of ice.

Snow

Hail

A VIOLENT SHOWER

You may have heard the expression "It's raining cats and dogs," but did you know that in some parts of England they used to say "It's raining cats, dogs and pitchforks"? The origins of both sayings are uncertain.

SNOW AND TEMPERATURE

If snow falls into extremely cold air, small, dry snowflakes known as powder snow form. Temperatures closer to zero tend to give rise to larger, wetter snowflakes that stick together easily—perfect for making snowballs!

THE SHAPE OF THE FLAKE

Snowflakes are tiny clusters of ice crystals. They form an infinite variety of shapes, which vary according to the temperature and humidity of the surrounding air.

25

Everchanging Colors

THE COLORS OF the sky are everchanging. Imagine a typical summer's day. You wake to a brilliant blue sky and dazzling white sunshine. By mid-morning, a few white, puffy clouds appear. Toward lunchtime, the clouds begin to swell, turning pale gray, slate, then almost black. After a heavy shower, a double rainbow arcs across the horizon. The clouds then clear and, as the light fades, the sky shifts through shades of yellow, gold, orange, red and purple.

Sunlight may look white, but it is actually made up of seven colors—red, orange, yellow, green, blue, indigo and violet. This color range is known as the spectrum. When we see all seven colors at once, they mix to form white. But certain elements in the atmosphere scatter, reflect and bend the seven colors. This means that we sometimes see only one color, or a mixture of a few, or several colors side by side.

Raindrops, for instance, split the spectrum so that we see seven bands of color. Water vapor and dust in the air scatter colors. Some are more easily scattered than others, so the sky changes color depending on the angle of the Sun and the amount of dust and water vapor. This process also creates an effect called a green flash, which occurs above the rising or setting Sun. As the Sun passes the horizon, the atmosphere splits its light and each color of the spectrum becomes briefly visible. The last one we see as the sun sets, or the first as it rises, is green, because blue, indigo and violet are always blocked by dust.

SHADES OF SKY
Water and dust in the air scatter the colors at the violet end of the spectrum more easily than those at the red end. So, when the Sun is high and the air is clear, a mix of violet, indigo, blue and green is spread across the sky, making blue. In the evening, when the Sun shines at a lower angle, sunlight has to pass through more dust and vapor and the colors toward the red end are scattered, making yellow, then orange and red.

HANDS ON

Create a Rainbow

1 Fill a wide basin with water. Place a mirror in the basin at an angle and hold it still. You may need to attach it to the bottom of the basin with modeling clay.

2 Place the basin so that the Sun shines through the water and onto the mirror. If you hold a sheet of white paper in front of the mirror and move it around slowly, you should eventually see a rainbow on the paper.

In the same way that raindrops bend and reflect the sunlight to form a rainbow in the sky, so the water and mirror are splitting and reflecting the light, enabling you to create a rainbow on the paper.

ELECTRIC LIGHTING
Spectacular streaks of colored light known as auroras sometimes appear in the skies over the North and South Poles. They occur when electrically charged particles generated by the Sun strike oxygen and nitrogen molecules in the atmosphere. The color of the aurora depends on the type of molecules the particles encounter.

All colors scattered equally

IT ALL ADDS UP TO WHITE
The water droplets in clouds scatter all the colors of white sunlight equally, so the color we see in the cloud is still white. Clouds appear gray or black only when they are in the shadow of another cloud or are blocking the light completely.

Word Builders

- **Aurora** comes from the name of the Roman goddess of the dawn.
- **Spectrum** was originally a Latin word meaning "appearance." The spectrum is the entire range of color that appears to our eyes.
- **Halo** comes from the Greek *halos,* meaning "disk of sun or moon."

That's Amazing!

- Rainbows usually disappear fairly quickly, but in Sheffield, England, on March 14, 1994, one remained visible for six hours, between 9 am and 3 pm, making it the longest-lasting rainbow ever recorded.

Pathfinder

- Auroras form in the highest level of the atmosphere. See pages 8–9.
- Learn to name clouds on page 22.
- Find out how the water droplets and ice crystals in clouds turn into raindrops on pages 24–25.

TRICKS OF THE LIGHT

Water droplets and ice crystals can split or bend white light so that it breaks up into the colors of the spectrum. This creates all kinds of weird and wonderful effects.

IRIDESCENCE
Sometimes water droplets in an uneven cloud create a patch of color called iridescence. The colors may slowly change as the cloud moves.

HALOES
When the Sun shines through a thin layer of high cloud made up of ice crystals, a colored ring or halo may appear in the sky around the Sun.

RAINBOWS
Raindrops not only break up sunlight, but reflect it. Each color is reflected at a slightly different angle, forming regular bands in the sky.

Wild Weather

page **30**
Why does the shape of this cloud indicate a mature thunderstorm?

Go to THUNDERSTORMS.

page **32**
Did you know that you can cook up a storm in your own kitchen?

Go to LIGHTNING.

EVERY SO OFTEN, our weather goes wild. Clouds darken, winds howl and lightning rips through the sky. Thunderstorms occur in most of the world, but some regions experience even wilder weather. In the tropics in summer, hurricanes threaten coastal areas, while in cold regions in winter snow and ice storms can wreak havoc. Even temperate areas can be devastated by the intense winds of tornadoes. Because such severe events cause widespread destruction and loss of life, scientists are constantly seeking ways to predict them and minimize damage.

page **34**
The funnel of a twister snakes toward the ground. But how does it form?

Go to TWISTERS.

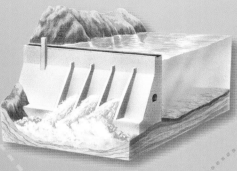

Thunderstorms

RUMBLING THUNDER AND brilliant flashes of lightning create one of nature's most awesome displays. To whip up a full-blown thunderstorm, our atmosphere requires various ingredients. The essential ones are warm, rising air currents, plenty of water vapor and low air temperatures at middle and upper levels of the atmosphere.

Warm, moist, rising air currents, or updrafts, carry the water vapor upward. As the moist air cools, the vapor turns into cloud. Because air keeps rising as long as it is warmer than its surroundings, the cloud continues to grow if the updrafts are warm and strong and the air at middle and upper levels is cold. Sometimes, when the air is rising rapidly, a small cap-like cloud called a pileus forms just above the main cloud. This is a clear sign that a storm is on its way.

A cumulonimbus, or thundercloud, can grow all the way up to the tropopause. There, it cools and spreads out, creating a wide, flat top known as an anvil. If the updrafts are very powerful, part of the cloud may punch through the tropopause, forming a bulge called an overshooting top.

Air in the upper part of the cumulonimbus then starts to sink, creating downward air currents called downdrafts. The combination of updrafts and downdrafts causes water droplets and ice crystals to grow and form rain and hail. It also creates the opposing electrical charges that cause lightning. When the downdrafts begin to outnumber the updrafts and the cold, sinking air cuts off the supply of warm, rising air, the storm weakens and the cloud breaks up.

INSIDE STORY
Rider on the Storm

There was nothing for it but to bail out. On July 27, 1959, US Marine Corps pilot William H. Rankin ejected from his damaged jet and opened his parachute. Within minutes, he found himself in "an angry ocean of boiling clouds"—a thunderstorm.

Again and again, Rankin fell, only to find himself being thrust aloft once more or hurled from side to side by powerful air currents. The temperature was far below freezing. Hail pummeled him and rain drenched him so much that he thought he might drown in mid-air. Thunder rattled his bones and lightning dazzled and scorched him.

After 40 minutes on this terrifying aerial roller-coaster, Rankin emerged from the cloud and floated to the ground. In doing so, he became the first American pilot to survive a parachute drop through a severe storm.

BUBBLING UNDER
Strange, bulging formations called mammatus clouds sometimes appear on the underside of a thundercloud's anvil. They occur when strong downdrafts push parcels of warm, moist air down into an area of cooler air. The moisture condenses and bubble-like clouds form. Because mammatus clouds are a sign of powerful air currents, airline pilots avoid flying through them.

Word Builders

• The top of a thundercloud is called an **anvil** because it looks like a blacksmith's anvil. The Latin for anvil is *incus* and this kind of cloud is called **cumulonimbus incus**.
• **Pileus** comes from the Latin word *pileus*, which means "felt cap."

That's Amazing!

• Approximately 2,000 thunderstorms are occurring around the world as you read this text.
• The town of Tororo, in Uganda, has the highest annual average number of days of thunder of any town on Earth. Between 1967 and 1976 Tororo experienced, on average, 251 thundery days each year.

Pathfinder

• Find out how water droplets and ice crystals turn into rain, snow and hail on pages 24–25.
• Read about lightning on pages 32–33.
• Thunderstorms can cause the most powerful winds. See pages 34–35.
• Take a flight into the eye of a tropical storm on page 36.

MULTICELL STORMS

A thunderstorm may consist of a single cloud or a cluster of clouds. The first type is called a single-cell storm and the second is a multicell storm. This dramatic photograph, taken by the space shuttle *Discovery*, shows a multicell storm over the Pacific Ocean near Hawaii.

WALL-TO-WALL THUNDER

This enormous cumulonimbus is bearing down on the city of Darwin in northern Australia. The wide, protruding edge at its base is known as a wall cloud. It is often a sign of a particularly severe storm that may bring torrential rain, strong winds and hail.

THE STORM CYCLE

Thunderstorms usually progress through three main stages. This entire cycle may take only 15 minutes or last for several hours.

BUILDING UP

Rising air currents carry water vapor upward into cooler air. The moisture condenses and a cumulus cloud forms.

AT ITS PEAK

The cumulonimbus grows to the tropopause then spreads out, forming an anvil. Air then begins to sink, creating powerful downdrafts.

ON THE WANE

The downdrafts begin to outnumber the updrafts. The storm's supply of warm, rising air is cut off. The cloud disintegrates, leaving a smaller cumulus cloud and some wispy cirrus clouds.

Lightning

WHAT MOVES AT 60,000 miles per second (96,600 kps), has a temperature of 50,000°F (27,600°C) and lasts just 1,000th of a second? Answer: a lightning bolt. Lightning is one of nature's most spectacular and fearsome forces. It is the result of a buildup of opposing electrical charges within a thundercloud. Scientists are not sure exactly how this occurs.

It is likely that the updrafts in a storm carry positive charges to the top of the cloud, and downdrafts drag negative charges to the bottom. These opposite charges are strongly attracted to each other. Eventually, the attraction becomes so great that electricity leaps, or discharges, from one area to the other. We see this as a bright flash or jagged white line—a lightning bolt. The intense heat generated by the charge causes the air to expand and contract rapidly, creating a loud bang that we call thunder. Because sound travels more slowly than light, we may not hear the bang for several seconds after we have seen the flash.

Most lightning occurs within a cloud. But negative charges at the bottom of a cloud may also be attracted to positive charges on the ground. Lightning may then strike open ground or tall objects. For this reason, you should move away from trees or high areas such as hilltops during a storm and try to find shelter indoors. You're safe inside a car as long as you don't touch any metal parts. At home, avoid using faucets or electrical equipment because charges from lightning may run along water pipes and power lines.

BALL LIGHTNING
Occasionally, lightning forms a ball that moves through the air then vanishes or explodes. This rare occurrence is ball lightning.

SOUND AND FURY
Though we see lightning as a single line or flash, the electricity actually moves rapidly backward and forward between the two charged areas an average of four times. This creates a flickering effect. You can estimate your distance from lightning by counting the number of seconds that separate the flash and the bang. Dividing that number by five gives the distance in miles (for kilometers, divide by three).

CLOUD-TO-CLOUD LIGHTNING
Lightning may jump within one cloud or between opposite charges in adjacent clouds.

BRANCHING OUT
Most lightning occurs within clouds, but bolts may strike out in other directions if opposite charges are present elsewhere. The three most common kinds of lightning are shown here.

Word Builders

• We sometimes see lightning as a widespread flickering in the sky. People call this **sheet lightning** but it is simply cloud-to-air or cloud-to-cloud lightning reflected in other clouds.

• As electrical charges build up in a storm, a cluster of sparks occasionally appears above tall objects under the cloud. Mariners first noted it above their ships' masts and called it **St Elmo's Fire**, for the patron saint of sailors.

That's Amazing!

• Lightning strikes Earth's surface about 100 times per second.

• There's no truth in the saying that lightning never strikes the same place twice. The Empire State Building, in New York, is hit about 500 times a year. In North America, around 400 people are zapped every year and one unfortunate person, Roy C. Sullivan, of Virginia, was hit a record seven times.

Pathfinder

• To find out more about clouds turn to pages 22–23.

• Powerful air currents called updrafts and downdrafts may be the source of lightning. See pages 30–31.

• More people are killed by lightning than by tornadoes. Forecasters therefore issue warnings if a storm is likely to be severe. See pages 56–57.

HANDS ON
Forked Lightning

You can make lightning using a plastic sheet, a metal bowl or pot, a rubber glove and a fork. The experiment works best in a dark room.

❶ Tape the plastic sheet to a table top.

❷ Wearing the rubber glove, pick up the bowl, then rub it briskly on the plastic sheet.

❸ Take the fork in your other hand and bring it close to the bowl. A spark will jump from the bowl to the fork.

As you rub the bowl on the plastic, a static charge builds up, just as it does in a thundercloud. When it comes near an object with the opposite charge (the fork), it immediately discharges, creating a mini bolt of lightning.

CLOUD-TO-GROUND LIGHTNING
If there is a positive charge on the ground, lightning may strike downward from the base of a thundercloud.

CLOUD-TO-AIR LIGHTNING
Electricity may move from the cloud to oppositely charged air.

Twisters

IT STARTS WITH AN enormous thundercloud. From its dense, black base, a funnel-like form snakes slowly toward the ground. As it touches down, a huge cloud of dust and debris billows outward. Objects hurtle through the air in all directions. The column swells as it comes closer, and a great roar rises like the sound of an approaching freight train. Time to take cover—there's a tornado on the way!

Also called a twister and a whirlwind, a tornado is one of the most powerful forces on Earth. This spinning column of air can measure up to 1 mile (1.6 km) in diameter, move at up to 65 miles per hour (105 kph) and generate winds of up to 300 miles per hour (483 kph). Often it is powerful enough to flatten houses and lift cars and people high into the air.

Tornadoes are most common in the United States, where more than 1,000 occur each year. The worst-affected region is a narrow belt known as Tornado Alley, which extends from Texas northward through Oklahoma, Kansas, Missouri and Nebraska. Several of the most devastating tornadoes have occurred here, including the deadliest, the Tri-State Tornado. On March 18, 1925, it tore eastward from Missouri for 219 miles (353 km) and killed 395 people.

Outside the United States, tornadoes are rarer. But if you think one is traveling your way, head indoors immediately. Go to a basement or a windowless interior room, get under a heavy piece of furniture and hang on tight.

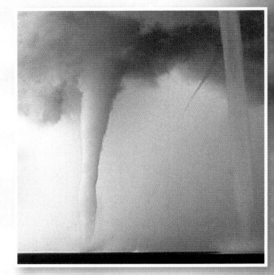

UP THE SPOUT
When tornadoes form over water, they create waterspouts. In place of dust, the rising air sucks up moisture which condenses to form a column of water. Waterspouts are usually weaker than tornadoes but can still overturn boats and kill or injure people.

A DEVIL OF A WIND
Weaker forms of whirlwinds can occur when crosswinds cause a rising air current to rotate. If the air picks up dust, it may become visible. This type of formation is known as a dust devil.

INSIDE STORY

The Chase Is On

For most people in Tornado Alley, the appearance of a huge thundercloud is enough to send them running for shelter. For Warren Faidley, it's a signal to grab his camera, climb into his reinforced truck and drive straight into danger. A full-time photographer of severe weather, Warren spends every spring pursuing tornadoes across the central United States.

He began chasing storms in 1988 after *Life* magazine published a photograph of lightning he had taken and christened him the "storm chaser." Soon he was obsessed by getting "the perfect tornado shot."

In May 1993, he managed to film seven tornadoes in a single day in Texas. In 1997, he filmed what was thought to be the first motion-picture footage of a real tornado. He has now taken thousands of spectacular images of twisters, which have been published all over the world. While

taking these pictures, Warren has been knocked off his feet by lightning and almost sucked out of a car by a tornado. But his desire to capture that perfect shot means that, despite the danger, the chase goes on.

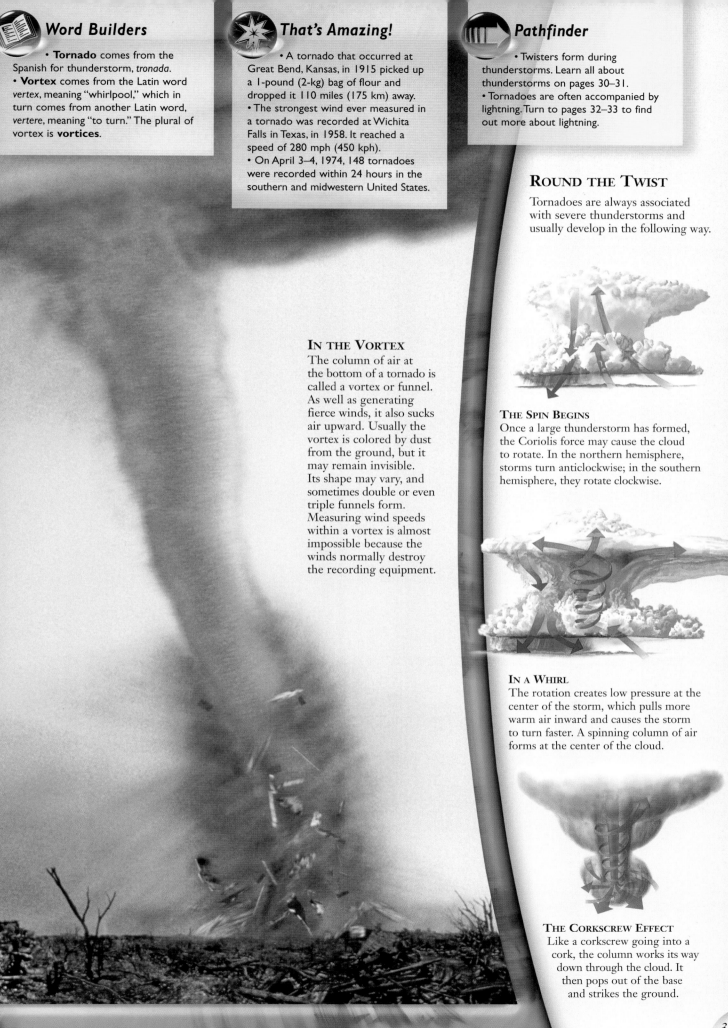

Word Builders

• **Tornado** comes from the Spanish for thunderstorm, *tronada*.
• **Vortex** comes from the Latin word *vertex*, meaning "whirlpool," which in turn comes from another Latin word, *vertere*, meaning "to turn." The plural of vortex is **vortices**.

That's Amazing!

• A tornado that occurred at Great Bend, Kansas, in 1915 picked up a 1-pound (2-kg) bag of flour and dropped it 110 miles (175 km) away.
• The strongest wind ever measured in a tornado was recorded at Wichita Falls in Texas, in 1958. It reached a speed of 280 mph (450 kph).
• On April 3–4, 1974, 148 tornadoes were recorded within 24 hours in the southern and midwestern United States.

Pathfinder

• Twisters form during thunderstorms. Learn all about thunderstorms on pages 30–31.
• Tornadoes are often accompanied by lightning. Turn to pages 32–33 to find out more about lightning.

ROUND THE TWIST

Tornadoes are always associated with severe thunderstorms and usually develop in the following way.

IN THE VORTEX

The column of air at the bottom of a tornado is called a vortex or funnel. As well as generating fierce winds, it also sucks air upward. Usually the vortex is colored by dust from the ground, but it may remain invisible. Its shape may vary, and sometimes double or even triple funnels form. Measuring wind speeds within a vortex is almost impossible because the winds normally destroy the recording equipment.

THE SPIN BEGINS

Once a large thunderstorm has formed, the Coriolis force may cause the cloud to rotate. In the northern hemisphere, storms turn anticlockwise; in the southern hemisphere, they rotate clockwise.

IN A WHIRL

The rotation creates low pressure at the center of the storm, which pulls more warm air inward and causes the storm to turn faster. A spinning column of air forms at the center of the cloud.

THE CORKSCREW EFFECT

Like a corkscrew going into a cork, the column works its way down through the cloud. It then pops out of the base and strikes the ground.

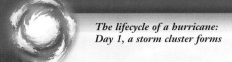

Hurricanes

A TORNADO MAY produce the strongest winds on Earth, but for destructive power nothing matches a hurricane—a huge spiraling storm system that forms over the ocean. It can measure up to 500 miles (800 km) in diameter and can produce torrential rain, winds of up to 190 miles per hour (300 kph) and an enormous high tide called a storm surge.

Hurricanes form over tropical oceans in summer. In southeast Asia they are known as typhoons and in the Indian Ocean and Australasia they are called cyclones. A hurricane begins as a cluster of thunderstorms near the equator. If the cluster drifts beyond five degrees north or south, it begins to rotate. The farther away from the equator it moves, the faster it spins and the more powerful it becomes. It qualifies as a hurricane when its wind speeds reach 74 miles per hour (119 kph). Amazingly, the calmest place in a hurricane is its center, or eye. This area of intense low pressure is usually free of cloud and strong winds.

If a hurricane strikes land, its storm surge and rains may flood large areas and its winds create a wide path of devastation. But when a hurricane leaves the sea, it also leaves behind its supplies of heat and moisture. So as it moves inland, it weakens rapidly and soon dies out.

INSIDE STORY

In the Eye of the Storm

Buckle up tight. It's going to be a bumpy ride. You just joined the 53rd Weather Reconnaissance Squadron on one of its regular flights from Mississippi, U.S.A., into the eye of a hurricane.

Two hours after takeoff, you reach the storm. The plane tilts and lurches through dark cloud. Rain and hail lash the windows. It's almost pitch dark, except for fearsome flashes of lightning. At the eye wall, the plane suddenly plummets. Your stomach seems to leap into your mouth. Then all at once, it's eerily still and silent. The Sun comes out. Peering up, you see blue sky. You're in the eye. After a couple of hours collecting data here, you'll be ready to head home.

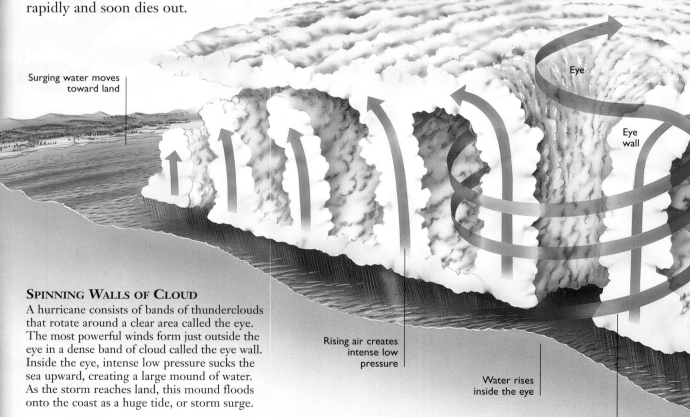

Surging water moves toward land

Eye

Eye wall

SPINNING WALLS OF CLOUD

A hurricane consists of bands of thunderclouds that rotate around a clear area called the eye. The most powerful winds form just outside the eye in a dense band of cloud called the eye wall. Inside the eye, intense low pressure sucks the sea upward, creating a large mound of water. As the storm reaches land, this mound floods onto the coast as a huge tide, or storm surge.

Rising air creates intense low pressure

Water rises inside the eye

Air spirals around the eye

Word Builders

- **Typhoon** comes from the Chinese *tai-fung*, meaning "great wind."
- In the 13th century, a typhoon destroyed a Mongolian fleet on its way to attack Japan. Believing the typhoon was sent to protect them, the Japanese called it *kami-kaze*, or "divine wind."

That's Amazing!

- It's impossible for a hurricane to cross the equator because there is no Coriolis Effect there. As a result, the system stops spinning and dies out.
- Hurricane Andrew, which struck Florida in the United States in 1992 caused US$26 billion of damage and was the most expensive natural disaster in American history.

Pathfinder

- Storms are fueled by warm, moist, rising air near the equator. Find out more on pages 12–13.
- Find out how rain forms inside a cloud on pages 24–25.
- To see an infrared image of a hurricane, turn to pages 52–53.

HEADS OR TAILS?
Powerful winds generated by hurricanes can flatten buildings, uproot trees and even flip objects as heavy as cars and boats.

STORM WATCH

When a hurricane is identified, it is given a name (male and female names are used alternately). From then on, it is monitored constantly by local weather bureaus.

PROGRESS REPORTS
Once a hurricane falls within the range of coastal radar units, it can be tracked and monitored by weather bureau staff.

UNPREDICTABLE ELENA
When Hurricane Elena arrived in the Gulf of Mexico in 1985, the US government evacuated 1 million people from Florida and Louisiana—the largest peacetime evacuation in American history. But the storm eventually came ashore in Mississippi and caused US$1.3 billion worth of damage.

Bands of thunderclouds

Illustration not to scale

A MODEL STORM
Radar and satellite data is used to create computer models. These help scientists assess the severity of the storm and issue appropriate warnings.

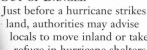

OUT OF DANGER
Just before a hurricane strikes land, authorities may advise locals to move inland or take refuge in hurricane shelters.

Floods

OF ALL THE KINDS OF weather-related catastrophes that occur, floods are the most destructive. They cause more deaths than any other type of natural disaster. They disrupt the lives of millions of people every year. And they result in billions of dollars of damage to property, crops and land.

There are three main kinds of floods: coastal, river and flash floods. Coastal floods occur when strong winds whip up high waves that swamp beaches and spill inland. Some of the most severe coastal flooding is generated by hurricanes, which can create enormous tides called storm surges.

River floods occur when rivers and other waterways overflow. This is usually the result of prolonged, heavy rainfall, often associated with an intense low-pressure system. Damage may be widespread, but the slow build up normally allows authorities to evacuate people and minimize loss of life.

Flash floods, on the other hand, occur quickly and are frequently deadly. They begin when a heavy downpour or a sudden release of water fills a narrow, sloping channel such as a canyon. The channel acts like a funnel, concentrating and speeding up the flow of the water. As the torrent races downward, it decimates everything in its path.

In areas that are prone to flooding, people build large structures to keep water out. These may make residents feel safer. But they can sometimes cause the very problem they were built to prevent. In many parts of the world, walls, dams and levees have collapsed suddenly, with disastrous results.

ALL WASHED OUT

In October 2000, torrential rain caused water torrents to engulf houses in Italy's north-east. Dams designed to trap floodwaters collapsed as water levels reached their highest point in over 30 years.

MISSISSIPPI BLUES

In 1993, torrential summer rains caused the Mississippi River in the central United States to burst its banks. About 12,000 square miles (31,200 sq km) of farmland were swamped and 52 people died. During the floods, emergency services used satellite images like this one to monitor the extent of the flooding.

FLOOD CONTROL

For thousands of years, humans have tried to reduce the risks of flooding by blocking and channeling the flow of rivers and oceans.

LEVEES

Rivers that regularly overflow or change course can be contained by building earthen embankments known as levees. Structures of this type have been used on the Huang River in China for more than 2,200 years. Sometimes, levees fail as a result of erosion, earthquakes or unusually high rainfall.

Word Builders

• **Levee** comes from the French word *lever*, meaning "to raise." A levee raises the level of a riverbank.
• A flood can also be referred to as an **inundation** or **deluge**. Inundation comes from the Latin word *unda* for "wave," and deluge is from the Latin *diluere*, meaning "to wash away."

That's Amazing!

• The worst-ever flood occurred on the Huang River in China in October 1887. It swamped 300 villages and killed at least 900,000 people, although some historians think the death toll could have been as high as six million.
• More people are killed in American deserts by floods than die of thirst.

Pathfinder

• Find out more about the causes of monsoons on page 13.
• As hurricanes near the coast they generate huge tides called storm surges. Learn more on pages 36–37.

GONE IN A FLASH
America's worst flash flood occurred on May 31, 1889, when the South Fork Dam, near Johnstown, Pennsylvania, gave way. A wall of water swamped the town, killing at least 2,200 people.

HANDS ON
Make a Rain Gauge

You can monitor rainfall by making a rain gauge.

❶ Ask an adult to help you cut the top third off a plastic bottle. Turn the top third upside down and place it inside the bottom two thirds to create a funnel.

❷ Take a tall, narrow glass jar and stick a strip of paper on one side.

❸ Pour water into the large bottle up to a height of half an inch or 1 cm, then pour this water into the narrow jar. Mark the water level on the strip of paper. Make a scale by marking increments of the same amount all the way up the strip. (The narrow jar makes it easier for you to measure smaller amounts.)

❹ Tape the bottle to a weight such as a brick and place it in an open area outside.

❺ At the same time each day, pour the contents of the large bottle into the narrow jar to measure how much rain has fallen.

TIDAL BARRIERS
In some low-lying coastal regions that are prone to flooding, such as southeastern England and the Netherlands, people have built large walls or barriers to control tides and block abnormally large waves.

DAMS
A dam is a concrete wall that blocks the flow of a river. It may be used to control rivers that are prone to flooding and to generate electricity by channeling the water through turbines. Dams must be very strong to support the large quantity of water that builds up behind them.

Camel train

Droughts

IF YOU LIVE IN AN ARID ZONE and hardly a drop of rain falls for a couple of months, you may think nothing of it. But in a more temperate zone, the same situation could qualify as a natural disaster—a disaster known as a drought.

In general terms, a drought is a period of unusually dry weather. But definitions vary around the world. In the United States, a drought is declared if less than 30 percent of normal rainfall has occurred in a three-week period over a wide area. In Australia, drought means 10 percent of normal annual rainfall.

It might take many months for a drought to develop. Once it takes hold, however, it can last for years. The immediate effects include water and food shortages and crop failures. In severe cases, these conditions may lead to famine and great loss of life.

Drought is normally the result of an unusual weather pattern. For instance, a change in wind direction could bring dry rather than moist air to an area, or abnormally high pressure may prevent the formation of cloud and rain. But such patterns may have other causes. Scientists now think that some droughts are the result of changes in sea-surface temperatures, which reduce the supply of moisture to the atmosphere.

LAND FILLS THE SKY
In a drought-affected region, normally moist soil becomes dry and loose. Strong winds may then lift the topsoil, creating an enormous moving cloud of dust called a dust storm. Such storms drastically reduce visibility and coat everything with a thick layer of grime. The dust may travel for thousands of miles and rise up to 10,000 feet (3,000 m) into the atmosphere.

INSIDE STORY

Dust Bowl Days

Times were good. The thousands of people who had migrated to the southern Great Plains of the United States in the early 20th century had found rich, fertile soil and a mild, wet climate. They had plowed up thousands of acres of grasslands and planted row upon row of crops. They lived well.

But, in 1931, times changed. The rain stopped and the soil began to dry and crack. The farmers thought it couldn't last. But years went by and no rain came. Drought spread across Colorado, Kansas, Oklahoma, Texas and New Mexico, a region that soon became known as the Dust Bowl. By 1937, when the writer John Steinbeck toured the area, it was the worst drought in American history. In his famous novel, *The Grapes of Wrath*, Steinbeck described the tragic scenes as countless farmers abandoned their homes and headed west in search of a better life: "Carloads, caravans, homeless and hungry; twenty thousand and fifty thousand and a hundred thousand and two hundred thousand. They streamed over the mountains … like ants scurrying for work, for food, and most of all for land."

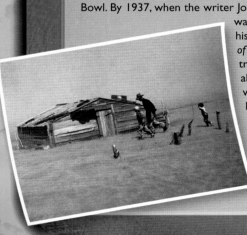

Word Builders

El Niño is a Spanish term and means "the boy." The opposite of El Niño is sometimes referred to as La Niña, meaning "the girl." Changes in air pressure across the Pacific Ocean caused by El Niño are known as the Southern Oscillation and are measured on a scale called the Southern Oscillation Index.

That's Amazing!

• The Atacama Desert in northern Chile is the driest place on Earth. It receives just a few local storms every 100 years or so.
• A drought in China in 1907 is thought to have caused 24 million deaths.
• The 1982–83 El Niño is estimated to have cost around US$8 billion worldwide.

Pathfinder

• El Niño disrupts normal air flow. Learn about air flow on pages 12–13.
• Dust storms are normally whipped up by cold fronts. Find out about frontal systems on pages 16–17.
• Find out how plants and animals cope with drought on pages 44–45.

DEVASTATED BY DROUGHT
Severe droughts brought famine to the Sahel region of North Africa in 1910–14, 1940–44 and 1970–85. Between 1972 and 1975, and again between 1984 and 1985, more than 600,000 people died.

THE EL NIÑO EFFECT

A warm sea current called El Niño may cause droughts in the southern hemisphere.

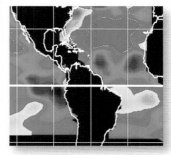

REGULAR WIND AND RAINFALL
This map depicts the normal ocean-temperature pattern across the Pacific Ocean, with warm water shown in red and cool water shown in blue. This results in close to average rainfall for most of the southern hemisphere.

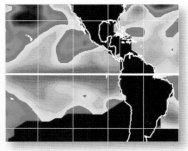

AN EL NIÑO YEAR
Every three to eight years, around December, El Niño moves down the Peruvian coast. This brings heavy rain to parts of western South America and results in dry weather in Australia.

KNOCK-ON EFFECTS
Parts of Australia may then suffer from drought. El Niño may also bring drought to northeastern Brazil and parts of Africa, and heavy rains to Argentina, Uruguay and southern Brazil.

Snow and Ice Storms

THERE'S SOMETHING MAGICAL about waking on the morning after a big snowstorm. Your world is transformed. Sun gleams off a spotless blanket of white. Icicles hang from roofs and fences, and frost sparkles on windows. And if you look closely, you'll see that every snowflake forms an intricate, exquisite pattern.

Snowstorms can be a source of wonder and a time for fun. But they also play havoc with our daily routine. Thick snow may block roads and disrupt emergency services. Low temperatures can endanger the lives of those without adequate heating or insulation, especially the old. Deep snow on mountainsides may lead to deadly avalanches.

Ice storms are just as dangerous. These occur when raindrops fall through freezing air but remain in liquid form. As soon as these "supercooled" droplets reach the ground, they freeze solid, coating every surface with a thick layer of ice. This makes roads and footpaths slippery and can cause widespread damage.

Snow and ice storms are usually produced by low-pressure systems in winter. Because these systems are so large and the temperature varies widely within them, it can be difficult for forecasters to predict if, where and when rain, snow or freezing rain will fall. One thing is certain, however: snow is more likely to fall in mountains, where temperatures are usually lower.

AFTER THE SNOW
America's worst snowstorm struck the east coast between March 11–14, 1888. About 5 feet (1.5 m) of snow fell and 400 people died. The damage bill came to US$20 million.

TYPES OF ICE
When supercooled raindrops strike a surface, they may spread out before they freeze. This forms a thick coating of clear, smooth ice called glaze, as shown in this photograph. If, on the other hand, the drops freeze immediately, they create a white, lumpy coating called rime. Rime is less slippery and therefore less dangerous than glaze.

AVALANCHE!
An avalanche is a large mass of snow that slides down the side of a mountain. Large avalanches can bury people, cars and even entire villages.

SLIPPERY WHEN WET
Avalanches often happen when a new fall of snow builds up on top of old, wet or icy snow, or when the snowbase begins to melt in spring.

Word Builders

• A severe snowstorm, especially one that involves strong winds, is often called a **blizzard**.
• In the United States, **sleet** is another word for frozen raindrops. But in the United Kingdom and Australasia the same word is used to refer to partially melted snowflakes.

That's Amazing!

• The people of Greenland have names for 50 different kinds of snow.
• The largest recorded snowflake fell in Montana, on January 28, 1887. It was 15 inches (38 cm) in diameter and 8 inches (20 cm) thick.
• The highest snowfall from a single blizzard occurred on February 13–19, 1959, at Mt Shasta, California. It measured 189 inches (480 cm).

Pathfinder

• Snow is often produced by low-pressure systems. Find out more about these systems on pages 16–17.
• Whether rain or snow falls depends on the temperature of the air near the ground. See pages 24–25.
• Plants, animals and humans have developed various strategies for coping with extreme cold and heavy snowfalls. Turn to pages 44–45.

INSIDE STORY

The Snowflake Man

He gently adjusted the focusing wheel on his new microscope and peered at the shape before his eyes. It was astonishing: a six-branched pattern of startling beauty. Who would have thought that such a marvel could exist in a single snowflake?

The study of snowflakes soon became a passion for 15-year-old Wilson A. Bentley of Vermont—one that would last a lifetime. Over the next 46 years, until his death in 1931, he spent thousands of hours examining their patterns. He would catch the flakes on a tray and carefully smooth them with a feather before photographing the most interesting specimens. Eventually, he published a book called *Snow Crystals*, which contained images of no fewer than 2,300 snowflakes. Each one, according to Bentley, was a "masterpiece of design." But the thing that really enthralled Bentley was that "no one design was ever repeated."

THE BIG FREEZE

Ice storms create extremely hazardous conditions. A thick coating of glaze makes it almost impossible to drive on roads or walk on footpaths. The weight of the ice can also bring down trees and power lines, and even upset the balance and performance of aircraft and sailing boats.

ON THE SLIDE

The snow may start to slide when it can no longer support its own weight. It can also be triggered by skiers or climbers. As the avalanche moves downhill, it begins to accelerate.

WAVE OF DANGER

The wave of snow may reach speeds of up to 155 miles per hour (250 kph) and flatten everything in its path. People buried by avalanches can stay alive for a short time under the snow, so rescuers often use sniffer dogs to locate survivors quickly.

Coping with Extremes

IN A WATERLESS DESERT, where the temperature regularly soars above 100°F (38°C), can any plant grow? In the snowy wastes of the Arctic, where land and sea freeze solid and it remains pitch dark for months, does any animal thrive? You may be surprised to learn that the answer to both questions is "yes."

Life has conquered almost every nook and cranny of our planet. Plants and animals—including humans—achieved this by slowly changing their behavior, and even their physical form, to suit particular environments. This process is called adaptation. Frequently, adaptation involves adjusting to extreme weather.

In the desert, some plants deal with drought by growing long roots that can reach water far underground. Most desert animals avoid the heat by staying in burrows by day and hunting at night when it is cooler. Some obtain water from plants or, as in the case of the darkling beetle of Namibia, from dew.

On the arctic tundra, plants grow low to the ground to shelter from wind, and flower quickly to take advantage of the short summer. Many polar creatures have thick fur and a layer of fat to keep them warm and some have white coats that camouflage them in the snow.

Humans, too, have developed physical characteristics to help cope with extreme environments. People who live in hot parts of the world usually have dark skin that protects them from strong sunshine. Inhabitants of the Arctic often have a thick layer of body fat that helps keep them warm.

STRATEGIES FOR SURVIVAL

Plants and animals have come up with a wide range of ingenious adaptations to extremes of weather. These include changes in behavior, size, shape and even color. This illustration shows examples of animal adaptations to extreme climates.

FRIENDLY FIRE
The banksia plants of Australia have adapted to the country's regular wildfires. Most species are fire-resistant and some cannot reproduce until fire opens their seeds.

DESERT The kangaroo rat of North America obtains all the moisture it needs from seeds and plants. It can live its whole life without drinking a drop of water.

TROPICAL Normally, tadpoles must stay in water. But in the rain forest, the air is so moist that the poison dart frog can carry its young on its back.

MOUNTAIN The pika of Asia and North America has thick fur that protects it from the cold. It survives winter by feeding on dried plants stored in its burrow.

Word Builders

- Many animals sleep through winter to avoid cold weather. This is called **hibernation**, from the Latin *hibernare*, meaning "to pass the winter."
- **Adaptation** comes from the Latin *adaptare*, meaning "to fit." Adaptation involves fitting into an environment.

That's Amazing!

- To quickly replace lost fluids, a camel can drink 30 gallons (136 l) of water in ten minutes.
- The emperor penguin of Antarctica can survive colder weather than any other creature. During winter, it endures temperatures of –80°F (–62°C) and winds of 120 miles per hour (190 kph).

Pathfinder

- Most of Earth's hot deserts are located around 30 degrees north or south of the equator. To find out why this is so, turn to page 12.
- Droughts occur in many regions other than deserts. Learn more about droughts on pages 40–41.

INSIDE STORY

High Flyers

"I hadn't realised just how much of a difference it makes. You can't see it, you can't feel it, you can't touch it." Like many other middle- and long-distance runners at the 1968 Olympics in Mexico City, Australian 10,000 m world-record holder Ron Clarke was shocked by the effect of the city's height of 7,573 feet (2,240 m) on his performance. Because there is less oxygen in the air at high altitude, runners from lower elevations struggle for breath. Prior to the Mexico Olympics, few athletes were aware of this. In the final of the 10,000 m, Clarke not only finished a disappointing sixth but also collapsed and had to be given oxygen. The race was won by Naftali Temu from the highlands of Kenya.

At the same time, athletes competing in sprints and jumps benefited from the thin air because it meant there was less wind resistance to short, quick movements. This is thought to have helped Bob Beamon achieve an incredible leap of 29 feet (8.9 m) in the long jump. That record was nearly two feet (0.7 m) longer than the existing record and remained unbeaten for the next 23 years.

HUMAN ADAPTATIONS

Humans have adapted to extreme weather through certain physical adaptations, but more often by wearing special clothes and building appropriate homes.

CHILLING OUT

The Inuit people of the Arctic wear clothes made of animal hides and build shelters called igloos out of blocks of ice. These structures minimize heat loss.

THE HIGH LIFE

To cope with reduced oxygen at high altitude, the Indians of the Andes mountains have larger-than-normal lungs that can inhale more air. They also have dark skin that resists sunburn.

STAYING COOL

Traditional peoples of the Sahara Desert move from place to place to find water. They wear loose-fitting robes that protect their skin and allow air to circulate.

POLAR
Dense fur and a thick layer of fat keep the polar bear warm. Its heart pumps warm blood to its skin to prevent it from getting frostbite.

Watching the Weather

GIVEN THE HUGE influence weather has on our lives, it is not surprising that humans have been trying to monitor and predict weather since the beginning of time. Early peoples attributed many weather phenomena to supernatural beings, but they also learned to recognize real patterns in weather and use these to predict general trends. It wasn't until the 16th century, however, that the study of weather became a true science. Since then, forecasters have devised sophisticated techniques and machines that help them make increasingly accurate forecasts.

page **48** Did you know that in Native American mythology the Thunderbird produces thunder, lightning and rain? What other myths attempt to explain the weather?

Go to LOOKING FOR SIGNS.

page **50** The invention of the telegraph and the Internet helped shape the history of meteorology.

Go to THE SCIENCE OF METEOROLOGY.

page **52** These thermometers measure temperature and humidity. Do you know how air pressure and wind speed are measured?

Go to MEASURING THE WEATHER.

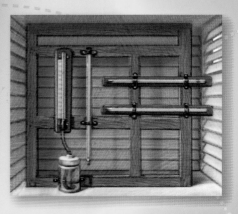

Mayan sun calendar

Looking for Signs

WHEN YOU WITNESS an awesome lightning display or a beautiful rainbow, it's not hard to understand why early peoples thought weather was the work of the gods. Many civilizations made up stories, or myths, to explain how supernatural beings created weather. Northern European, or Norse, peoples, for instance, believed that a god called Thor created thunder by striking his hammer. Some cultures performed prayers, dances and sacrifices to please their gods and bring better weather. The Mayans of medieval Mexico threw gems, gold and humans into wells as an offering to their rain god, Chac.

Other people looked for more rational explanations for the weather. Farmers and sailors especially devised sayings that linked changes in the weather with other natural signs. These sayings, or weather lore, were passed down from generation to generation, and many are still in use today. Some are simply superstitions—there is no truth in the old American saying "when birds and badgers are fat in October, expect a cold winter." But others contain a grain of truth—"clear moon, frost soon" refers to the fact that cold, clear nights are usually followed by frost.

THUNDERBOLT CITY
In ancient Greek mythology, Helios was the god of the Sun and Aeolus was the god of the wind. But the most important weather deity was Zeus, the ultimate ruler of the heavens, who controlled clouds, rain and thunder. Myths describe how he would create storms by hurling great bolts of lightning from his seat atop Mount Olympus, said to be the home of the gods.

THE LIGHTNING MAN
This rock art in northern Australia depicts a figure from Aboriginal myths—Namarrgon, the Lightning Man. A band of lightning runs around his body, and he uses the stone axes on his head, elbows and knees to strike the clouds and create thunder.

WINGS OF THUNDER
A mythical bird known as the thunderbird appears at the top of many Native American totem poles. In Native American mythology, the thunderbird creates thunder by flapping its giant wings and produces lightning by flashing its eyes.

Chinese dragon, symbol of seas and rains

Word Builders

- Sayings and proverbs relating to weather phenomena are known collectively as **weather lore**. The word *lore* comes from the Old English word *leornian*, meaning "to learn."
- **Hopi** is a Native American word that means "good" or "peaceful."

That's Amazing!

- A ground-dwelling African bird called the guinea fowl starts to build a nest when a storm is on the way. It has been proved that the guinea fowl can sense thunder hundreds of miles away, so this behavior is a reliable sign of an approaching storm.
- Ants sense rain long before it begins, and will often start raising the level of the earth around the entrance to their nest to prevent water entering.

Pathfinder

- Many superstitions were inspired by optical effects, such as rainbows and haloes. See page 27.
- When animals or plants appear to be behaving in an unusual way, it may be that they are responding to extreme weather. See pages 44–45.

INSIDE STORY

Dancing for Rain

The dancers stand in a circle before the priest, and place live snakes in their mouths. The priest steps forward and strokes each snake with an eagle feather. So begins the Snake Dance, a ritual performed every two years in August by the Hopi people of the southwestern United States. They believe that the dance encourages rain to fall and water their crops. Preparations for the ritual take many days. The dancers fast, then go out to gather snakes. Prior to the ceremony, Hopi women care for the snakes, feeding and washing them like honored guests.

The dance takes place in the kiva, an underground chamber. Smeared with colored clay and wearing feathered headdresses and skirts bearing a snake motif, the dancers circle the kiva. Each one carries one or more snakes, sometimes in his mouth, sometimes over his shoulder. At the end of the ceremony the snakes are released, to carry the Hopis' prayers to the rain gods.

WEATHER LORE

Certain natural signs are said to predict changes in the weather. This is seldom true, although they may accurately reflect current conditions.

DAMP DETECTOR

Some people say that open pine cones indicate fine weather. Pine cones close when the air is damp, so open cones are a sign of dry air.

A SHEPHERD'S DELIGHT?

The saying "Red sky at night, shepherd's delight" suggests that a clear western sky in the evening will be followed by a fine day. This is true at times, but only where the weather usually comes from the west.

FIELD STUDIES

Many people believe that if cows sit down, bad weather will follow. When rain starts, cows do often sit down to keep a patch of grass dry.

WEB REPORT

The presence of many spider webs is said to be a sign of good weather. This is untrue, though spiders do stop weaving their webs during heavy rain.

STORM BREAKER

This wooden staff was carved by the Yoruba people of Nigeria. It is an image of their god of thunder, Shango, who creates storms by flinging thunderbolts down to Earth from the heavens. During special ceremonies, Yoruba priests held up staffs like this one to ward off violent storms.

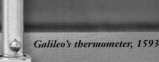

Early barometer modeled on Torricelli's

Leonardo's hygrometer, ca 1500

Galileo's thermometer, 1593

The Science of Meteorology

PEOPLE BEGAN TO study weather scientifically over 2,000 years ago. Around 300 BC, for example, Indian scholars measured rainfall using the first rain gauges, and Chinese astronomers recorded how the weather changed from season to season. In Greece, the philosopher Aristotle (384–322 BC) wrote a book called *Meteorologica* which attempted to describe all known kinds of weather. It included many accurate observations and coined a name for the scientific study of weather—meteorology.

Some significant developments in meteorology occurred in Italy during the 16th and 17th centuries. The astronomer and mathematician Galileo Galilei (1564–1642) invented the first thermometer and one of his pupils, Evangelista Torricelli (1608–47), made the first barometer. Scientists at the Academy of Experiments in Florence used these devices to set up the first weather observation network in 1654.

Soon, other national networks were founded. But one major problem with these networks was that by the time information was gathered it was out of date. This was overcome in 1837 when Samuel Morse invented the telegraph. Using this method of rapid communication, forecasters could receive news of changing conditions before the changes arrived.

In the last 50 years, the introduction of radar and satellites, as well as computers able to process large quantities of data, has helped meteorologists produce more accurate forecasts.

COLLECTING DATA

In the early 20th century, meteorologists began to use pilotless aircraft such as kites and balloons to collect data from the upper atmosphere. This weather kite was built by French scientist Teisserenc de Bort. It was launched from his observatory in Paris during the First World War.

NUMERICAL FORECASTING

In 1922, British scientist Lewis Fry Richardson suggested that weather forecasts could be calculated using mathematical equations. But the calculations required were extremely complex and it wasn't until 1950 that a successful numerical weather forecast was made, using this early computer called ENIAC.

GIANT STEPS

The science of meteorology has evolved gradually and benefited from the contributions of thousands of scientists. But certain developments resulted in major leaps forward.

Fourth century BC
Aristotle writes *Meteorologica*

1593 Galileo invents thermometer

1643 Torricelli makes first barometer, which also demonstrates the existence of air pressure for the first time

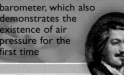

Word Builders

• **Meteorology** comes from the Greek words *meteoron*, meaning "something high in the sky," and *logos*, for "study."
• **ENIAC** stands for Electronic Numerical Integrator And Computer.

That's Amazing!

• In the era before computers, Lewis Fry Richardson estimated that producing a single numerical forecast would require 64,000 mathematicians, each equipped with a calculator.
• ENIAC weighed over 30 tons, had about 6,000 switches and filled a room.

Pathfinder

• Teisserenc de Bort discovered the stratosphere. See page 8.
• Hygrometers measure humidity. Find out how to make one on page 21.
• Satellites play a major role in monitoring weather conditions. Learn more on pages 52–53.

EYE IN THE SKY

The launch of TIROS I (Television Infrared Observation Satellite) on April 1, 1960, transformed meteorology. For the first time, forecasters could receive regular pictures of cloud over a large area. This in turn allowed them to monitor storms.

NAMING THE WINDS

The ancient Greeks defined eight winds according to their direction and named them after gods. Each god is sculpted on the appropriate side of this building in Athens. Known as the Tower of the Winds, it was constructed in the first century BC.

HANDS ON

Barometer in a Bottle

The barometer was one of the most important developments in meteorology. Make your own by following these simple instructions.

❶ Stretch a piece of balloon across the top of a can or jar. Attach it firmly so no air can get in or out.

❷ Cut one end of a plastic drinking straw to make a point. Tape or glue the other end across the top of the container.

❸ Tape a piece of card to the side of the container near the pointer. Mark the position of the pointer on the card, then check it and mark it again the next day. When the air pressure is high, the pointer will move down. When it is low, it will rise.

1837 Morse invents telegraph

National weather services founded in U.K. and France (1854) and U.S.A. (1869)

1935 Invention of radar, which allows meteorologists to monitor severe storms and precipitation

1951 Formation of World Meteorological Organization increases global cooperation

1990s Development of Internet revolutionizes distribution of information

Measuring the Weather

WEATHER ISN'T JUST to do with temperature and rainfall. It's also about air pressure, wind speed, humidity and even ocean currents. To build up a complete picture of current and future weather, meteorologists measure all of these things, and more. This involves gathering data from many levels—from the surface to the tropopause and beyond.

On the ground, meteorologists measure local conditions with a range of instruments, including thermometers to register temperature, hygrometers to record humidity and barometers to measure air pressure. These are placed at weather stations across a wide area. Until recently, observers had to go to the stations to collect data. But now many stations are Automatic Weather Stations (AWSs), which record automatically and transmit to meteorologists via phone, radio and satellite.

In the upper atmosphere, meteorologists use piloted and remote-controlled aircraft. Balloons tow aloft tiny instrument packages called radiosondes to heights of up to 100,000 feet (30,000 m). Radiosondes record air pressure, temperature and humidity. Even farther above the Earth, satellites take and transmit photographs of cloud cover at regular intervals. Some also carry equipment that can record temperatures and wind speeds at various levels of the atmosphere, while others can even measure ocean currents and the heights of waves on the sea.

EYE IN THE SKY
Research aircraft can carry a wide range of weather-monitoring instruments into the upper atmosphere. This plane flies into the center of hurricanes to gather data for computer models.

BEAUFORT SCALE	This scale, which was devised in 1805, is sometimes used to estimate wind speeds.			
CODE	SPEED (MPH)	SPEED (KPH)	DESCRIPTION	EFFECTS ON LAND
0	below 1	below 1	calm	smoke rises vertically
1	2–3	1–5	light air	smoke drifts slowly
2	4–7	6–11	light breeze	leaves rustle; vanes begin to move
3	8–12	12–19	gentle breeze	leaves and twigs move
4	13–18	20–29	moderate breeze	small branches move; dust blown about
5	19–24	30–38	fresh breeze	small trees sway
6	25–31	39–51	strong breeze	large branches sway; utility wires whistle
7	32–38	52–61	near gale	trees sway; difficult to walk against wind
8	39–46	62–74	gale	twigs snap off trees
9	47–54	75–86	strong gale	branches break; minor structural damage
10	55–63	87–101	whole gale	trees uprooted; significant structural damage
11	64–74	102–120	storm	widespread damage
12	above 74	above 120	hurricane	widespread destruction

HEAT SEEKER
This infrared satellite image shows the eye of a hurricane. Infrared sensors detect heat rather than light, so the colors indicate the temperatures of cloud tops. The dark red color near the center highlights the lowest temperatures. These are produced by the tops of large thunderstorms which form a ring around the eye of the hurricane.

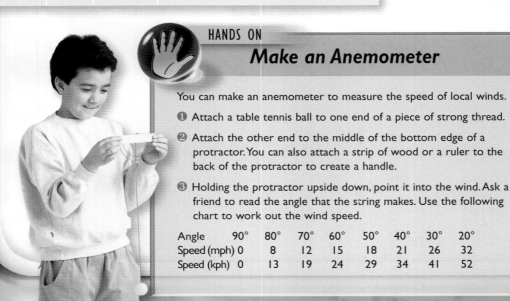

HANDS ON

Make an Anemometer

You can make an anemometer to measure the speed of local winds.

❶ Attach a table tennis ball to one end of a piece of strong thread.

❷ Attach the other end to the middle of the bottom edge of a protractor. You can also attach a strip of wood or a ruler to the back of the protractor to create a handle.

❸ Holding the protractor upside down, point it into the wind. Ask a friend to read the angle that the string makes. Use the following chart to work out the wind speed.

Angle	90°	80°	70°	60°	50°	40°	30°	20°
Speed (mph)	0	8	12	15	18	21	26	32
Speed (kph)	0	13	19	24	29	34	41	52

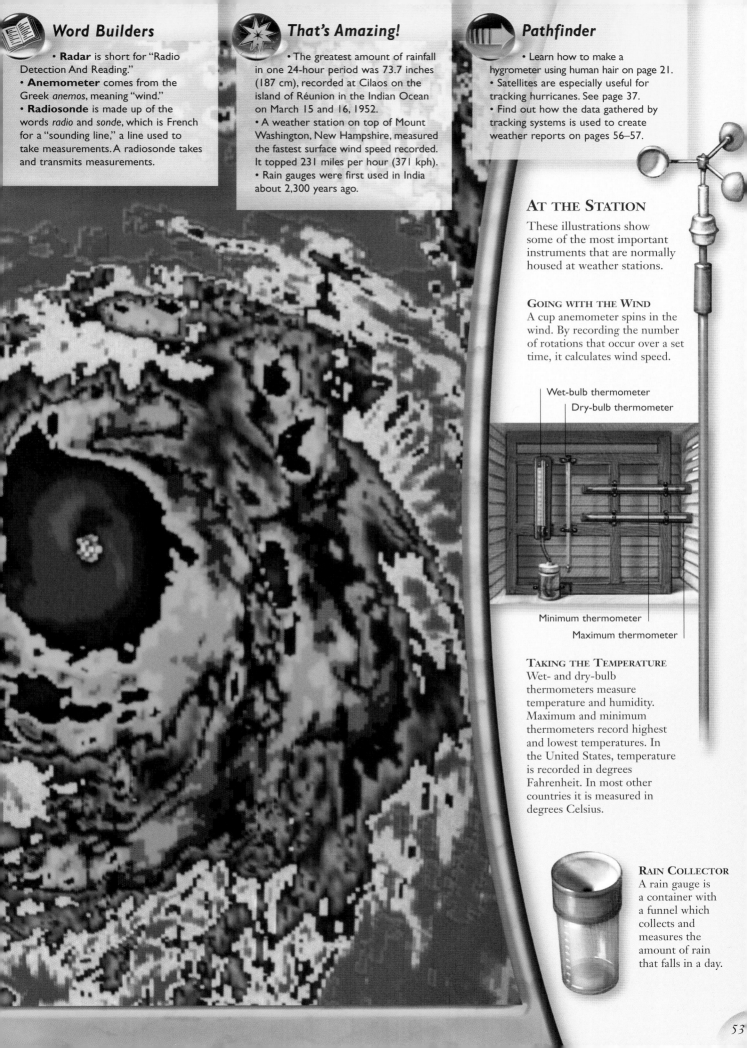

Word Builders

- **Radar** is short for "Radio Detection And Reading."
- **Anemometer** comes from the Greek *anemos*, meaning "wind."
- **Radiosonde** is made up of the words *radio* and *sonde*, which is French for a "sounding line," a line used to take measurements. A radiosonde takes and transmits measurements.

That's Amazing!

- The greatest amount of rainfall in one 24-hour period was 73.7 inches (187 cm), recorded at Cilaos on the island of Réunion in the Indian Ocean on March 15 and 16, 1952.
- A weather station on top of Mount Washington, New Hampshire, measured the fastest surface wind speed recorded. It topped 231 miles per hour (371 kph).
- Rain gauges were first used in India about 2,300 years ago.

Pathfinder

- Learn how to make a hygrometer using human hair on page 21.
- Satellites are especially useful for tracking hurricanes. See page 37.
- Find out how the data gathered by tracking systems is used to create weather reports on pages 56–57.

AT THE STATION

These illustrations show some of the most important instruments that are normally housed at weather stations.

GOING WITH THE WIND

A cup anemometer spins in the wind. By recording the number of rotations that occur over a set time, it calculates wind speed.

Wet-bulb thermometer

Dry-bulb thermometer

Minimum thermometer

Maximum thermometer

TAKING THE TEMPERATURE

Wet- and dry-bulb thermometers measure temperature and humidity. Maximum and minimum thermometers record highest and lowest temperatures. In the United States, temperature is recorded in degrees Fahrenheit. In most other countries it is measured in degrees Celsius.

RAIN COLLECTOR

A rain gauge is a container with a funnel which collects and measures the amount of rain that falls in a day.

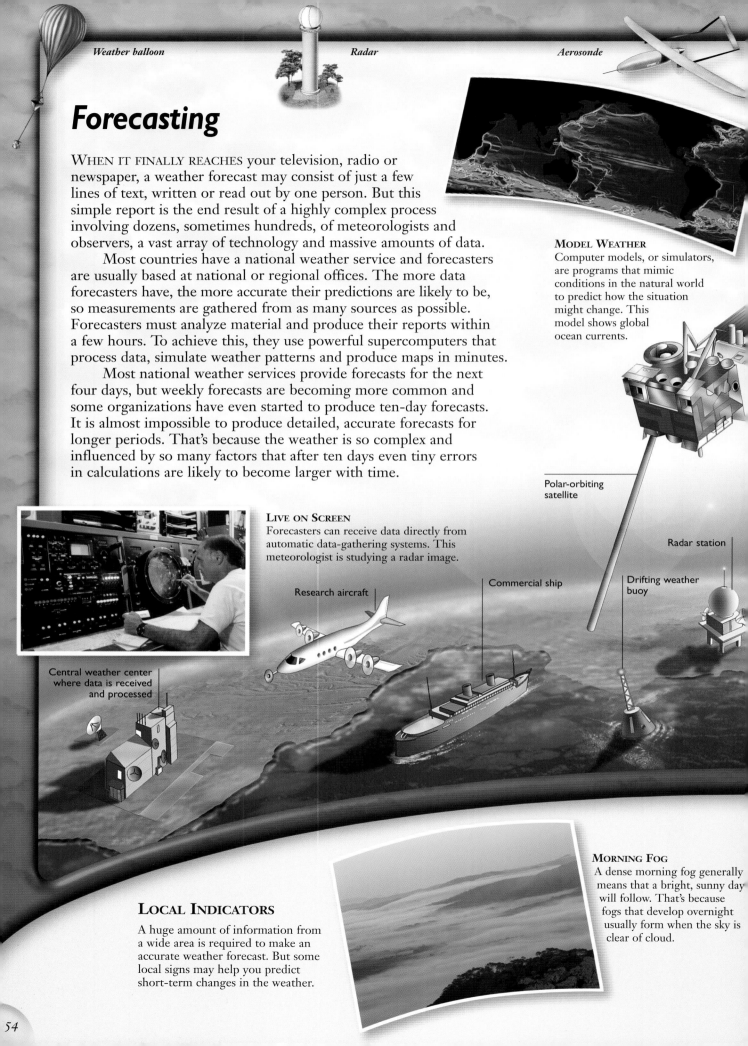

Forecasting

WHEN IT FINALLY REACHES your television, radio or newspaper, a weather forecast may consist of just a few lines of text, written or read out by one person. But this simple report is the end result of a highly complex process involving dozens, sometimes hundreds, of meteorologists and observers, a vast array of technology and massive amounts of data.

Most countries have a national weather service and forecasters are usually based at national or regional offices. The more data forecasters have, the more accurate their predictions are likely to be, so measurements are gathered from as many sources as possible. Forecasters must analyze material and produce their reports within a few hours. To achieve this, they use powerful supercomputers that process data, simulate weather patterns and produce maps in minutes.

Most national weather services provide forecasts for the next four days, but weekly forecasts are becoming more common and some organizations have even started to produce ten-day forecasts. It is almost impossible to produce detailed, accurate forecasts for longer periods. That's because the weather is so complex and influenced by so many factors that after ten days even tiny errors in calculations are likely to become larger with time.

MODEL WEATHER
Computer models, or simulators, are programs that mimic conditions in the natural world to predict how the situation might change. This model shows global ocean currents.

Polar-orbiting satellite

LIVE ON SCREEN
Forecasters can receive data directly from automatic data-gathering systems. This meteorologist is studying a radar image.

Radar station

Research aircraft

Commercial ship

Drifting weather buoy

Central weather center where data is received and processed

MORNING FOG
A dense morning fog generally means that a bright, sunny day will follow. That's because fogs that develop overnight usually form when the sky is clear of cloud.

LOCAL INDICATORS

A huge amount of information from a wide area is required to make an accurate weather forecast. But some local signs may help you predict short-term changes in the weather.

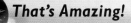

Word Builders

• A **geostationary** satellite remains stationary, or in a fixed position, over one spot on Earth's surface (*geo* is Greek for "earth" or "ground"), usually somewhere near the equator. In contrast, a **polar-orbiting** satellite constantly circles Earth, normally via the poles.
• The word **simulator** comes from the Latin word *simulare*, meaning "to copy" or "to represent."

That's Amazing!

• A supercomputer can carry out more than 1 billion mathematical calculations per second.
• Some satellites can transmit up to 150,000 observations every day.
• The World Weather Watch coordinates the exchange of data between national weather organizations. It gathers measurements from 12,000 weather stations, 7,000 seacraft, 700 radiosonde operators and hundreds of aircraft.

Pathfinder

• Significant alterations in air pressure are usually a clear sign of changing weather. Read more about air pressure on pages 10–11.
• Forecasters keep a close eye on developing frontal systems. Find out why on pages 16–17.
• Weather forecasts are usually presented in the form of maps or charts. Learn how to read a weather map on pages 56–57.

Geostationary satellite

HANDS ON

Recording the Weather

By keeping regular records, you will become aware of the most common weather patterns in your area. This, in turn, may help you forecast some short-term changes in conditions.

You can use the instruments you have made—the barometer (page 51), rain gauge (page 39) and anemometer (page 52)—to record air pressure, rainfall and wind speed. You should also measure the air temperature using a thermometer, and check the wind direction using a weather vane. Note all the measurements in a journal or logbook and use the symbols on page 57 to record extra information such as cloud types.

It's also a good idea to draw or take photos of interesting phenomena such as cloud formations or optical effects. Stick the pictures into your journal to create a fascinating visual record of the local weather.

THE REPORTING CYCLE

Every few hours, data is collected and forwarded to weather centers by the devices shown here. Forecasters must then process this information and create reports in the form of maps, charts and written bulletins. As soon as the process is finished, it starts all over again.

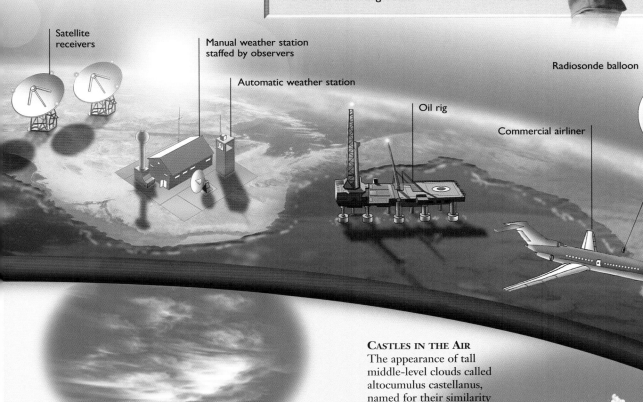

Satellite receivers

Manual weather station staffed by observers

Automatic weather station

Oil rig

Radiosonde balloon

Commercial airliner

CASTLES IN THE AIR
The appearance of tall middle-level clouds called altocumulus castellanus, named for their similarity in shape to castle turrets, is a sign that thunderstorms could develop.

HIGH CLOUD
The arrival of a band of high cloud may indicate the approach of a frontal system. If so, it will be followed by thicker cloud and possibly rain.

Weather Reports

FORECASTERS NORMALLY produce two kinds of weather maps: synoptic and prognostic. A synoptic map is a snapshot of the weather as it was when the measurements were taken. A prognostic map predicts how the weather will be in the future—say, in 12 or 24 or 48 hours. Both types of map are created with lines and symbols that are used and understood by meteorologists all over the world.

To inform the general public, weather bureaus supply television channels, radio stations and newspapers with simplified versions of these maps. They also provide reports directly to the public via phone, fax and Internet services. Some of these reports are customized for people whose jobs or hobbies are directly influenced by changes in the weather, such as pilots, sailors, farmers and climbers.

An important function of weather reports is to advise people of severe weather events. During the hurricane season in the United States, for example, forecasters issue a "hurricane watch" if there is a chance of a hurricane striking an area within the next 36 hours. If a hurricane is expected within 24 hours, they send out a "hurricane warning." This tells people to leave the coastline and head inland. Alerts like these play a crucial role in protecting property and limiting loss of life all over the world.

STATUS REPORT
This forecaster is creating a synoptic chart by hand. He records measurements received from weather stations and draws lines to mark frontal and pressure systems. The map will be used to predict subsequent changes in conditions.

HANDS ON
World Wide Weather

By logging onto the World Wide Web, you can track the weather in your region and in almost any other part of the world. There are hundreds of weather-related web sites that you can visit, and most national meteorological organizations supply regularly updated online weather reports.

In the United States, for example, the National Weather Service provides Internet weather reports for every part of the country. Go to www.nws.noaa.gov and look under "Current Conditions" then select your state and town. You can also obtain weather information from sites run by commercial organizations such as The Weather Channel (www.weather.com).

Children all over the world use the Internet to participate in the GLOBE program. Under this scheme, students and teachers gather information about the weather and other aspects of the environment in their area and send it to a central archive. In turn, they can find out about conditions in other parts of the world and communicate with meteorologists and other scientists. For more information, take a look at www.globe.gov.

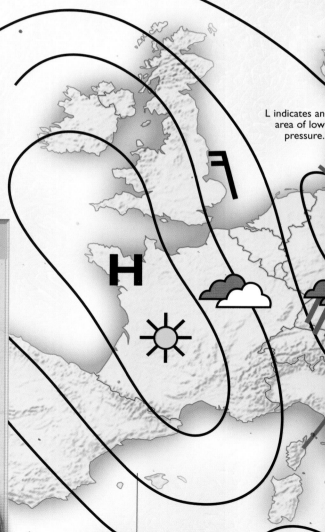

L indicates an area of low pressure.

Lines called isobars link points with the same air pressure.

This is the symbol for a cold front.

Light wind

Word Builders

• **Synoptic** comes from the Greek word *synoptikos*, meaning "a general view of the whole."
• **Prognostic** comes from the Greek *prognostikos*, meaning "foretelling."
• **Isobar** comes from the Greek words *iso*, meaning "equal," and *baros*, meaning "weight." An isobar links points of equal atmospheric, or air, pressure, which is the weight of the air.

That's Amazing!

• Forecasters must issue alerts with care. When a hurricane warning is issued on the Gulf Coast of the United States, all businesses must close. This costs the economy about US$50 million.
• On May 3, 1999, more than 200 tornadoes ripped through the central United States. Early warnings issued by local authorities are estimated to have saved approximately 700 lives.

Pathfinder

• Differences in pressure are the cause of winds. See pages 10–11.
• In midlatitudes, the wildest weather tends to occur on fronts. Learn more about frontal systems on pages 16–17.
• The data required to produce a weather map come from a wide range of sources. Turn to pages 54–55.

READING A WEATHER MAP

Although weather maps you see on television and in newspapers are usually less complex than those used by forecasters, they include some of the standard symbols shown in the panel on the right. The lines on the map below are called isobars. They link areas of equal air pressure, so the closer the different isobars are the greater the pressure difference and the stronger the wind in that area.

DIGITAL WIZARDRY

Most weather maps are now produced by computers. This weather map of Australia was created by superimposing a computer-generated chart on top of a color-enhanced satellite photograph. The yellow and red areas indicate the highest clouds.

WEATHER SYMBOLS

Meteorologists use a set of internationally recognized symbols to create maps. The most widely used symbols are shown here.

Current Weather

drizzle	
rain	
snow	
hail	
freezing rain	
tornado	
dust storm	
fog	
thunderstorm	
lightning	
hurricane	

Clouds

stratus	
stratocumulus	
cumulus	
cumulonimbus incus	
altostratus	
altocumulus	
altocumulus castellanus	
cirrus	
cirrostratus	
cirrocumulus	

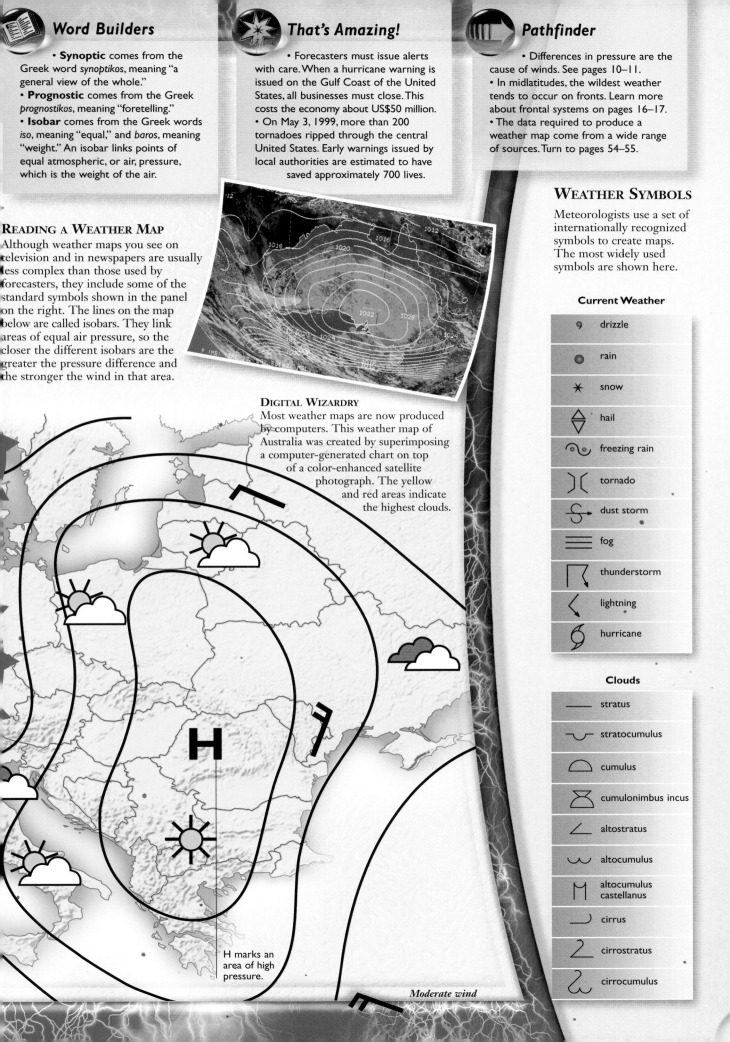

H marks an area of high pressure.

Moderate wind

The bases of icecaps contain ancient deposits of dust and gases that reveal what the weather was like up to 220,000 years ago. To obtain samples, scientists extract long columns of ice called ice cores.

Ice core

Every year a tree adds another ring to its trunk. These rings can be clearly seen when the trunk is cut. A wide ring indicates a warm, wet year whereas a narrow ring is a sign of a cold, dry year.

Tree rings

The Big Picture

SCIENTIFIC WEATHER RECORDS date back 300 years. They show that during this time our climate has hardly changed. But other records reveal that on a much larger scale—one measured in millions of years—our climate has been anything but constant.

During several phases of Earth's history, temperatures were much lower, and up to one-third of the land was covered by ice. There have been several of these cold phases, or ice ages, in the last 1.6 million years, each lasting thousands of years. Between each ice age, there were warmer periods called interglacials. We are living in an interglacial that began about 10,000 years ago.

Evidence for these changes comes from many sources. Among the most important are fossils. Because certain plants and animals can only survive at particular temperatures, some fossils are a good guide to temperature fluctuations in the past. Other sources of climate data include tree rings and ice cores.

The reasons for climate change are unclear, however. Earth's landmasses have drifted around over millions of years, and this may have altered weather patterns. Or it may be that tiny fluctuations in the planet's orbit vary the amount of sunlight reaching Earth. But we have little idea what the weather will be like in 1,000 or even 100 years from now.

PUTTING IT ALL ON ICE

Between 1450 and 1850—a period known as the Little Ice Age—winters in Europe were especially severe. In London, the surface of the River Thames froze over regularly. From 1607 onward, Londoners took advantage of these conditions to hold events called frost fairs. The last frost fair took place in 1814.

Depending on the severity of the frost, the ice could be up to 18 feet (6 m) thick.

INSIDE STORY

Signs of Ice

As he hiked across high peaks of his native Switzerland in 1836, Louis Agassiz became fascinated by the effects of the country's many glaciers on the surrounding landscape. Valleys that contained glaciers had a distinctive U-shape and their walls were lined with grooves where the ice had scraped stones against the rock. But what most intrigued Agassiz was that he had seen these signs elsewhere—in places where glaciers did not exist.

Four years later, Agassiz published a book called *Studies on Glaciers*. In it he suggested that large areas of Earth had once been covered by glaciers during cold periods he referred to as "ice ages." But like many great scientists, Agassiz was ahead of his time. When he died in 1873 he had few supporters, and it wasn't until the end of the century that the concept of ice ages became widely accepted.

A CLIMATE TIMELINE

This timeline shows the major climate changes that have occurred during Earth's 4.6-billion-year history. The wavy line on the chart indicates the temperature relative to today's average, which is marked by the straight horizontal line.

3,700 mya Climate 18°F (10°C) warmer than today

330 mya Start of long ice age

2,700–1,800 mya Ice sheets widespread

450 mya Brief ice age

245 mya Climate warms; dinosaurs appear

Present average temperature   mya = million years ago   ya = years ago

Word Builders

• The study of prehistoric climate is known as **paleoclimatology**. This word comes from the Greek terms *palai*, meaning "long ago," *klima*, for "climate," and *logos*, meaning "word."
• **Fossil** comes from the Latin *fossilis*, meaning "obtained by digging," which in turn comes from *fodere*, "to dig."

That's Amazing!

During the early part of the warm period known as the medieval climatic optimum, which began around AD 900, about 400 people from Iceland established a settlement in Greenland. The population grew to around 5,000. But as the weather turned colder during the 12th and 13th centuries, crops began to fail. Soon the colony ran out of food, and in the 15th century it was finally abandoned.

Pathfinder

• Learn more about Earth's orbit around the Sun and how it affects the planet's climate on pages 10–11.
• Today, only mountaintops and polar regions are permanently covered by ice. Find out more about the Earth's current climate zones on pages 18–19.
• Could we be changing the climate? Find out on pages 60–61.

Stalls and booths were set up. They sold food and drink and even souvenirs of the ice fair.

CELESTIAL SUNBLOCK
Every 150 million years or so, Earth's orbit takes it through dust lanes in the arms of the Milky Way. These may block sunlight, causing atmospheric cooling and even ice ages.

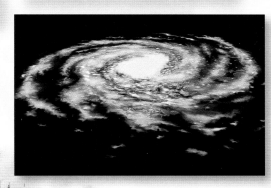

COOLING SYSTEM
Volcanoes spew enormous quantities of ash and gases into the air, which can block the Sun and reduce temperatures. In prehistoric times, large eruptions may have led to ice ages. Today, they may cause the climate to cool for months.

65 mya Gradual cooling begins; dinosaurs vanish

1.6 mya Cooling continues; ice ages occur roughly every 100,000 years

Brief, warm interglacial periods occur between ice ages

18,000 ya Peak of last ice age

6,000 ya Warm climate encourages birth of farming

AD 900–1100 Warm period called medieval climatic optimum

1450–1850 Little Ice Age

59

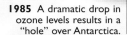

Changing the Weather

RECENT REPORTS SUGGEST that certain human activities may be altering Earth's climate. These changes could spell trouble for us and our planet.

In the last century, global temperatures rose by 1°F (0.6°C). This global warming, as it is known, may be due to an increase in greenhouse gases. These gases occur naturally in the atmosphere and keep our planet warm by trapping heat reflected by Earth's surface. But the burning of fossil fuels such as oil and coal, which are used to run cars and to provide most of our electricity, is creating extra greenhouse gases. This may in turn be causing the atmosphere to overheat. If this goes on, ice caps could melt, seas rise and large areas of farmland could become desert.

Other practices are damaging the ozone layer, a layer of gas in the stratosphere that protects us from harmful solar radiation. Industrially produced chemicals called chlorofluorocarbons (CFCs), which are used in aerosols, refrigerators and air conditioners, have destroyed some of the ozone. This has allowed more radiation to reach us and may be causing an increase in skin cancer and eye diseases.

Whether we realize it or not, we all contribute to these problems. That means we can all help prevent them—by buying CFC-free products and by minimizing our energy use or switching to alternative sources such as solar and wind power. In these and other ways we can limit the damage being done to the atmosphere and help preserve our natural environment, for our benefit and the benefit of future generations.

1985 A dramatic drop in ozone levels results in a "hole" over Antarctica.

2000 The hole is the largest ever recorded, extending northward over South America.

POINT OF WEAKNESS
The "hole" in the ozone layer is an area of greatly reduced ozone that appears over Antarctica between August and October every year. Since it was first discovered, it has gradually grown larger, almost certainly as a result of the continued use of CFCs and other chemicals. (Blue indicates low levels of ozone, while red shows high levels.)

SOMETHING IN THE AIR
Large cities such as Mexico City generate enormous amounts of air pollution. This forms a thick haze known as smog. Smog can be harmful to human health, create acidic gases that erode buildings and contribute to global warming.

Word Builders

- The word **smog** was made up from the words *smoke* and *fog*. Before the introduction of smokeless fuels, smoke produced by burning coal was the main cause of smog. Today, emissions from cars and factories are the most significant sources.
- **Ozone** comes from the Greek *ozein*, meaning "to smell." Ozone has a very strong smell.

That's Amazing!

- For every 1 percent of ozone that is destroyed, there is a 2 percent increase in the amount of harmful ultraviolet radiation reaching Earth.
- Some scientists think Earth's temperature could rise by as much as 10°F (6°C) over the next 100 years.

Pathfinder

- Find out more about the functions of the ozone layer and greenhouse gases on page 9.
- Global warming is likely to increase the frequency of major floods. Learn more about floods on pages 38–39.
- Learn how scientists study long-term changes in climate on pages 58–59.

HOTTING UP

The more the temperature of the atmosphere increases, the more dramatic the effects of global warming are likely to be.

WETTER WEATHER
A warmer atmosphere will result in increased precipitation and floods. Global rainfall levels have already risen by about 1 percent in the last century.

A HARD RAIN
The burning of fossil fuels fills the air with chemicals that mix with water vapor to form acid rain. Acid rain kills plants, poisons animals and waterways, and destroys vital nutrients in soil.

1990 The hole covers all of Antarctica and remains in place until December.

RISING SEA LEVELS
Warming causes glaciers and icecaps to melt, which in turn raises sea levels. In the past 100 years, sea levels have risen 6–8 inches (15–20 cm) around the world.

INSIDE STORY

A Hole in the Sky

In 1974, the world wasn't listening. American scientists Mario Molina and Sherwood Rowland had published an extraordinary article, which predicted that the use of CFCs would create a hole in the ozone layer. But other researchers cast doubt on their claims, and industrialists and politicians just didn't want to know.

In 1985, however, researchers at the British Antarctic Survey base in Antarctica (below, right) recorded such a dramatic drop in ozone levels that at first they thought their instruments were faulty. The hole that Molina and Rowland had predicted was now present.

The British findings made governments finally sit up and take notice. In 1987, countries belonging to the United Nations signed the Montreal Protocol, which banned the use of many dangerous CFCs. And in 1995, Molina and Rowland's foresight was recognized at last, when they were awarded the highest scientific honor in their field, the Nobel Prize for Chemistry.

DESERTIFICATION
Higher temperatures will make semiarid regions arid. That could turn some farmland into desert and result in food shortages.

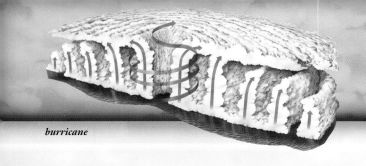

Glossary

acid rain An acidic form of rain that occurs when chemicals produced by the burning of fossil fuels mix with water vapor in the air.

aerosonde A small, pilotless aircraft used for recording weather data.

altitude Height above sea level.

alto The prefix used to describe the cloud formations which occur between 6,000 feet (2,000 m) and 16,500 feet (5,000 m).

anemometer A device used to measure the speed of wind.

anvil The top of a thundercloud.

atmosphere The ocean of air that surrounds Earth.

atmospheric pressure The weight of the air above a point on Earth's surface.

aurora A spectacular streak of colored light which occurs when electrically charged particles generated by the Sun strike oxygen and nitrogen molecules in the atmosphere.

Automatic Weather Station (AWS) A weather station which automatically records and transmits data via phone, radio and satellite.

avalanche A large mass of snow that slides down the side of a mountain.

barometer A device used to measure atmospheric pressure.

Beaufort scale A scale devised by William Beaufort in 1805, and used to estimate wind speeds.

blizzard A very severe snowstorm with especially strong winds.

Celsius The unit of measurement used to record temperature in most countries.

chlorofluorocarbons (CFCs) Industrially produced chemicals used in aerosols, refrigerators and air conditioners.

cirro The prefix used to describe cloud formations which occur above a height of 16,500 feet (5,000 m).

climate The pattern of weather that occurs in a region over an extended period of time.

coalescence The merging of water droplets within cloud to form raindrops.

condensation The cooling process by which water vapor becomes liquid.

convection A lifting of air caused by heating of the ground by the Sun.

Coriolis Effect The deflection of wind patterns by the rotation of Earth.

crosswinds Winds blowing at an angle to the direction of movement of a system.

dam A wall that blocks the flow of a river. It may be used to control flood-prone rivers and to generate electricity by channeling water through turbines.

desertification The process by which fertile land turns into desert as a result of decreasing rainfall.

downdrafts Downward-moving air currents.

dust storm A huge moving cloud of dust.

El Niño The warm sea current which arrives off the Western coast of South America about every seven to ten years and may cause droughts in the southern hemisphere.

environment The physical and biological circumstances that surround us.

evaporation The process by which heated water turns into water vapor.

eye The clear area of intense low pressure in the center of a hurricane.

Fahrenheit The unit of measurement used to record temperature in the United States.

flash flood A sudden, rapid flood caused by the channeling of a large mass of water through a narrow space such as a canyon or river valley.

fog Cloud that forms in a layer close to, or on, the ground.

forecaster A person who analyzes weather data and predicts weather patterns.

fossil The remains, trace or impression of any living thing preserved in, or as, rock.

fossil fuels The remains of organisms or their products embedded in the earth, with high carbon and hydrogen contents. These include fuels such as oil and coal.

front The boundary between two air masses of different temperatures.

glaze A thick coating of clear, smooth ice.

global warming An increase in the average temperature of the atmosphere.

gravity The force by which bodies are attracted to Earth.

green flash The effect caused as the atmosphere scatters sunlight near sunrise or sunset. Each color of the spectrum becomes briefly visible and the last color is green, because blue, indigo and violet are always blocked by dust.

greenhouse gases Gases that prevent heat escaping from Earth's atmosphere.

Gulf Stream An ocean current that carries warm water from the Caribbean Sea to the North Atlantic Ocean.

barometer *cold front symbol* *cumulonimbus with anvil and mammatus*

ozone layer   *weather balloon*   *temperate vegetation*

hectopascals A unit of measurement used to record air pressure. There are 100 pascals in a hectopascal.

hemisphere One half of the Earth. Europe and Northern America are in the northern hemisphere, while Australia and South America are in the southern hemisphere.

humidity The amount of water vapor in air.

hurricane A huge spiraling storm system that forms over tropical oceans in summer.

hygrometer A device used to measure humidity.

ice age A cold phase in the climatic history of Earth, during which large areas of land were covered by ice.

interglacial Period between ice ages.

inundation Another name for a flood.

iridescence Irregular patches of color in the sky caused by the bending of light around water droplets.

isobar A line on a weather map that links points of equal atmospheric pressure.

latitude A measurement of distance from the Equator.

levee An earthen embankment built to block or channel the flow of a river or ocean.

meteorology The scientific study of weather.

Milky Way The galaxy in which our solar system is located.

molecule The smallest particle into which a substance can be divided without it becoming something else.

monsoon A seasonal wind which produces heavy rains in tropical and subtropical zones.

Nobel Prize An annual prize awarded at the bequest of Alfred Nobel. The Nobel Prize is the highest honor in many fields of science.

ocean current A movement of sea water caused by global wind patterns. Ocean currents can carry warm and cold water long distances around the globe.

ozone layer The thin layer of ozone gas, located roughly 15 miles (24 km) above Earth's surface, which shields us from ultraviolet rays generated by the Sun.

precipitation Water droplets and ice crystals falling to Earth as rain, hail or snow.

prevailing winds The most consistent wind patterns for an area.

prognostic map A map predicting future weather patterns.

radiosonde A tiny instrument package towed aloft by a balloon. It records air pressure, temperature and humidity.

rain shadow A comparatively dry area on the sheltered side of a mountain range, created by the drying out of air masses as they cross the range.

rime A white, lumpy coating of ice.

St Elmo's Fire The appearance of a cluster of sparks above a tall object during a thunderstorm, caused by a buildup of electrical charges.

spectrum The entire range of color that appears to our eye—red, orange, yellow, green, blue, indigo and violet.

storm surge The wave that crashes onto the coast as a hurricane reaches land. It forms as a mound of water in the eye of the hurricane.

stratosphere The atmospheric level above the troposphere.

synoptic map A chart that shows the weather at a particular time.

temperate Regions which are neither very hot nor very cold. Temperate areas have four distinct seasons.

thermometer An instrument for measuring temperature.

tornado A spinning column of air that can measure up to 1 mile (1.6 km) in diameter, move at up to 65 miles per hour (105 kph) and generate winds of up to 300 miles per hour (482 kph).

tropopause The boundary between the troposphere and the stratosphere.

troposphere The lowest layer of the atmosphere. This is the layer in which we live and in which approximately 99 percent of our weather occurs.

updrafts Rising air currents.

virga Rain that evaporates before it reaches the ground. Virga is often visible as streaks in the sky.

vortex The spinning funnel of a tornado.

water vapor Water in the form of gas.

waterspout A spinning column of water-filled air that forms when air currents suck water upward from a lake or ocean.

weather balloon A balloon used to carry meteorological instruments.

weather bureau The place where weather data is collated and analyzed before being supplied to television channels, radio stations and newspapers.

weather lore Sayings and proverbs, often passed down over many generations, that relate to weather phenomena.

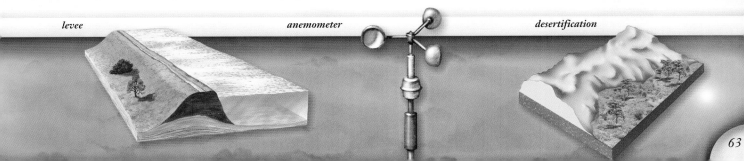

levee   *anemometer*   *desertification*

Index

The publishers would like to thank the following children who feature in the photographs: Charlotte Barge, Alex Hall, Cassandra Hall, Eloise Hall, Heide-Jo Kelly, Emily Knight, Gregory Knight, Elizabeth Lum, Abbey Piaud, Christopher Piaud, Jules Smith-Ferguson, Pasang Tenzing.

PICTURE CREDITS
(t=top, b=bottom, l=left, r=right, c=center, f=flap, F=Front, C=Cover, B=Back).
AAP Images 42bl. **AdLibitum** 5bc, 7br, 11cl, 12tc, 14bl, 18c, 20b, 21bl, 26bl, 28c, 32l, 39br, 47cr, 51br, 52bl, 55r, 56bl (Mihal Kaniewski). APL 13tr, 14br, 18tr, 20c, 21br, 26tl, 27br, 27cr, 30bl, 31t, 32-33c, 37br, 37c, 39tr, 40bl, 41cr, 42c, 42tr, 45c, 51cr, 54cl, 59br (Corbis); 17tc, 25bl. **Bill Bachman** 57t. **Digital Stock** 37tl. **Warren Faidley** 34bc. **Hurricane Hunters USA** 36c. **Getty Images** 34bl (Tony Stone/Buff Corsi); 34tr (Tony Stone /Dr Scott Torquay); 10tr (FPG); 8bl (Hulton Archive); 12bc, 37tr (Tony Stone); 35l, 61tr. **NASA** 47bt, 60-61c (GSFC-SVS, TOMS Project). NGS 32cl (W. Faidley). 53l. **NOAA** 61bc (Photograph by Dr. Ryan Sanders), 43cl. **Photo Essentials** 49tr. **photolibrary.com** 59tr (Baun and Hembest/SPL); 24b, 26tr (Jocelyn Burt); 60bl (Conor Caffrey/SPL); 27l (Jack Finch/SPL); 54tr (Los Alamos Nat. Lab/ SPL); 22bl (Magrath/Folson); 22c (NASA); 8tr (NASA/ Goddard SPC Flight/ SPL); 16tl (NASA/Science Source); 37tr (NASA/SPL); 27tr (George Post/SPL); 12cl, 15br, 17c, 38bl, 50bl, 56tr, 8cr (SPL); 9bl (Van Sant/GEO/SPL); 10cl (Robin Smith); 25br, 58bl, 61tc. **Physical Oceanography Research Division, Scripps Institute of Oceanography** 41tr, 41cr (Warren B. White). **Royal Meteorological Society, London** 22bc. **San Diego Historical Society Photograph Collection** 24cl. **Dr. P.S.C Tacon** 48l. **Wildscape Australia** 52tr (Peter Jarver) 30-31c, 54b.

ILLUSTRATION CREDITS
Anne Bowman 29bl; 44/45. **Chris Forsey** 4tr; 6br; 7bl; 14/15c; 14tl; 14tc; 14tr; 15bl; 15bc; 24/25; 29t; 36/37; 62tl. **Richard McKenna** 47tr; 54/55; 60/61; 63tc; 63br. **Nicola Oram** 7tr; 18t; 18/19b; 63tr. **Oliver Rennert** 1tr; 3tr; 5tr; 6bl; 6tcr; 6bcr; 10/11; 12/13; 28tr; 28bl; 28br; 30/31; 32/33; 34/35; 46bl; 46br; 52/53; 62bl; 62br; 62bc; 63bc. **Glen Vause** 4br; 4tcr; 7cl; 20/21; 26bc; 29cl; 40/41; 46t; 46c; 48/49; 50/51; 62tr. **Laurie Whiddon** 14cr; 16cr; 18/19c; 47cr; 56/57. **Wildlife Art Ltd.** 4cr; 6tc; 7c; 7tl; 8/9; 16/17b; 16tl; 16tc; 17r; 22/23; 29br; 29cr; 38/39; 42/43; 47cl; 58/59; 63tl; 63bl.

COVER CREDITS
Chris Forsey FCtcl, FCc, FCbr, BCtcl. **Richard McKenna** FCbc, BCcr. **Oliver Rennert** FCbcl, FCbcr, FCcl, FCbl, Fft, BCbr, BCbcl, Bfb. **Glen Vause** FCtl, Ffb, BCbl, BCtr, BCtl, Bfc. **Wildlife Art Ltd.** FCtr, FCbg, Ffc, BCbc, Bft.